T0336295

Advance Praise for *The Quintessential Good Samaritan*

"Fellow-healer John Kelly devoted his life to the physical, emotional, and psychological healing of the socially and racially disadvantaged. His story inspires in these troubled times."

—Deepak Chopra

"John Kelly lived his life helping Black and minority lives matter, ahead of his Christian church and ahead of the current social movement. John's life story in *The Quintessential Good Samaritan* is a heartfelt template of racial fairness and equity. Kelly's dedication to those in need and his compassion for all, lifted and inspired me and those around him who witnessed his extraordinary contributions to humanity."

—Susan Manheimer, former San Mateo and Oakland, California Chief of Police

The
QUINTESSENTIAL
GOOD SAMARITAN

The Authorized Biography *of*
John Joseph Kelly,
Champion *of* Social Justice

THOMAS HUENING

Post Hill
PRESS

A POST HILL PRESS BOOK
ISBN: 978-1-63758-128-5
ISBN (eBook): 978-1-63758-129-2

The Quintessential Good Samaritan:
The Authorized Biography of John Joseph Kelly, Champion of Social Justice
© 2022 by Thomas Huening
All Rights Reserved

This is a work of nonfiction. All people, locations, events, and situations are portrayed to the best of the author's memory.

Post Hill Press
New York • Nashville
posthillpress.com

Published in the United States of America
1 2 3 4 5 6 7 8 9 10

To: Carol, Monica, Jennifer, Melissa and Natalie
and for a world of kindness and compassion

A Good Samaritan is not simply one whose heart is touched
in an immediate act of care and charity,
but one who provides a system of sustained care.
James A. Forbes,
The first African American to be appointed as Senior Minister
of the Riverside Church in Harlem

Contents

FOREWORD

John Kelly was a saint—an irreverent saint who refused to play by rules that made no sense and prevented him from offering shelter, food, and healthcare for those in pain. He was never politically correct but always correct in his politics. I admired him more than words can communicate. I always felt like I was in the presence of a holy man who pushed the limits of human goodness.

As these thoughts are being written, the world is in the grips of a mighty pandemic. I wonder what John would say if he were here today. I have an inkling. While the captains of industry shake and ask for government assistance, John would ask for help for the poor. While the powerful delay questions of state due to partisan differences, John would counsel us to first pay attention to the welfare of children and then to rest assured that all else would be resolved accordingly.

I read an article recently that asked if politicians lie all the time or just some of the time. It was a disheartening question, but not an uncommon sentiment in our times. John was quite different. He inspired politicians to be better than they thought they could be and when that didn't work, he embarrassed them to the same end. Woe be to anyone of authority who failed to look John in the eye or who stumbled in their commitments to those with no means for, assuredly, they would know their own weakness from John's calm judgment.

Samaritan House was and remains John's gift of generous spirit to one of the most dynamic communities on the planet. If we truly believe in equal opportunity, then John's great masterpiece and his enduring legacy will be that this gift teaches the community how to turn the ideal of equal opportunity into reality each day. It's an important lesson for a community that might otherwise slip into soulless self-absorption born of historic wealth.

Thank you, John, for your spirit and the institution that it built. Our community may survive on water from the Sierra Nevada mountain range, but we thirst for the humanity and humility that you bequeathed as your example.

U.S. Congresswoman Jackie Speier (D), California

INTRODUCTION

One warm August day in 1979, fifty-one-year-old Father John Joseph Kelly ended his formal Mass at St. Mark's Catholic Church in Belmont, California, turned to the crowd, and in his booming baritone voice, wished all the ritual "Peace of the Lord."

The congregants in this makeshift parish south of San Francisco dutifully echoed their expected response: "And also with you." Kelly then softly asked people to shake hands as the traditional sign of peace. He paused a long while, gazing at the packed audience, ready to take a life-changing step into an uncertain future—one he could have never believed possible years earlier.

Slowly, Kelly reached to the hem of his vestment, pulled it up over his head, and held the gold-trimmed white silk cloth just a moment before dropping it in a clump at his feet. He straightened to his full six-foot-two height and looked to the parishioners as if a hundred pounds had been lifted from his shoulders. He saw several parishioners fighting back tears, each shocked that after twenty-five years as a priest, Kelly was renouncing his days as a devout man of the cloth.

Now, dressed simply in a sport shirt and trousers, he was just one of them, no longer their spiritual guide to the Jesus Christ he worshipped on a daily basis. To mark the occasion, one of joy for him, he softly began to sing the song "Born Free," and the congregation immediately joined in. When the singing ceased, many parishioners rushed to Kelly, and for several minutes, they hugged him with love in their hearts. Some others turned and left in disapproval.

For months, Kelly had wrestled with his conscience, hoping he could fulfill his vocation and continue the Catholic life he had chosen so long ago. But after witnessing the shortcomings of modern religion and after a long and painful struggle, he discovered he could not budge the Catholic bureaucracy to accept his form of social action. Finally, the conflict of emotions had led him to this day of decision, to leaving his Mother Church behind in this disobedient, shocking, yet personally satisfying final act.

To be certain, Kelly had become a "fallen-away" former Roman Catholic priest. He hadn't quit to be married or been defrocked because of a scandal. Rather, his advocacy for social justice for the poor and oppressed exceeded and transcended that of his church. He felt his commitment had been coopted by the organizational, bureaucratic model that plagues many organizations that have grown too large.

Kelly would never say it, but he had become holier than his Church by simply following the example of how Jesus lived his life. His inspiration led to a life of true inclusion and caring for everyone in need with no exceptions, examples that had been part of the early organizational church. Kelly didn't fall away from his belief in Jesus. He leapt away from a distorted image of Jesus with clear purpose and passion for compassion that he couldn't find in his Church.

In the days and weeks ahead, there would be no miracles or lightning bolts of instant enlightenment. Kelly struggled with each life choice like other mortals. First, he focused only on survival without a plan to be or do good. Fortunately, others saw his potential and helped animate him into a life dedicated to social justice. He soon recognized all the human needs around him and set about fulfilling those needs as his job and his life's work.

Fulfilling these human needs led Kelly to become not unlike Jesus, St. Francis of Assisi, Mother Teresa, and Mahatma Gandhi. During a life dedicated to others who had lost their way and needed his love, he would be instrumental in helping feed thousands of people who were hungry, providing them shelter, and making certain they had adequate clothing. Then, when these tasks were completed, he would become a true saint to lost, imprisoned souls through his tireless efforts in the area of restorative justice at San Quentin Prison and the county jail near his home.

Without question, John Kelly was an unglorified hero, a role model, and a champion for social justice for anyone who truly desires to make a difference in today's confusing world. From his very lips to my ears and from those who knew him best, this is his remarkable story.

Tom Huening

Priest and Teacher

In 1953, there were two ways for an Irish Catholic boy
to impress his parents:
become a priest or attend Notre Dame.
Phil Donahue

ONE

Growing Up in San Francisco

JOHN KELLY WAS not born a saint, and by age three, beleaguered by his older brother Ray, he often cried, whined, and screeched. In March 1932, his mother, Elly, bringing home baby number three, gave up trying to control his tantrums and decided to send him away. Four-year-old John cried and shrieked as he headed away to his exile. Told to be happy and proud of his new baby brother, he instead felt rejected, sad, and lonely. He was delivered to godmother Nora Kyne from San Francisco across the Bay to the city of Oakland to ease Elly's added burden of new son number three. He didn't realize that he caused his mother's distress, that he brought on his own banishment, that the move was temporary, or that he'd soon be allowed back home.

Mother Elly, five-six, slender, and nice looking with a head for numbers, felt increasingly trapped and burdened by motherhood and seeing her dream of a business career slip further away.

She'd only completed eighth grade but worked as a bookkeeper for the Magnavox company.

Elly regretfully had to turn down a head bookkeeper promotion offered when the company division relocated from the Bay area to the Midwest. She was smart, but her earlier education had been stalled due to her family's failing financial circumstances, which had caused them to immigrate to the U.S. from Norway.

With added son Donald, post-partum Elly felt overwhelmed and defeated in her efforts to control John as she struggled day by day just to get by. Nora, on the other hand, enjoyed her godson's stay and gave him undivided attention. After three months, his mother said she was ready to take on the extra load, and John's godmother returned him home.

The time seemed brief to the adults, but to John, three months was an eternity. Upon arriving back home, he wondered whether he still belonged to the family and worried they wouldn't allow him to stay. His mother, occupied with baby Donald and older son Ray, still had little time for John, which amplified his insecurity. He resumed acting like a brat. Meanwhile, his father Raymond was distant and left childrearing mostly to Elly. John felt his tall Irish dad didn't know or care what was going on in his troubled family.

Shortly after his return home, John needed a thyrotoxic cyst removed, and his overnight hospital stay intensified his feeling of abandonment. By late age four, he started having nightmares and "spooky dreams." He began a new pattern of even angrier, screaming tantrums.

Elly, already frustrated with the demands of raising her family, was unsympathetic and demanded that John stop crying. His acting out was a constant disturbance in her life, but she had few solutions as to how to make him behave. Exasperated, she settled on trying to intimidate him in a most unusual and detrimental way: Elly told him he wasn't a boy at all; he was really a girl. She insisted that since boys wouldn't whine and cry and sulk like he did on a daily basis, he must not really be a boy.

Young John was unable to associate his misbehavior with his mother treating him so badly. One day after whining and throwing yet another tantrum, she grabbed a bucket of water and chased her son down the narrow space alongside their home. He reached the end where he couldn't reach a high gate latch and became trapped. She cornered John and dumped cold water over him, hoping to shock him into better behavior. At her wits' end, she figured that was the only way she could make her wayward son stop acting up. To further punish him, she directed him to go downstairs to the basement while still soaking wet, and she ignored the boy for a long time.

When her shock therapy failed, Elly became even more exasperated with her son's rebellious conduct. She put him in one of her dresses and forced him to walk out in the backyard by himself. Crying all the way, he ranted and raved while walking around humiliated in his mother's dress, not realizing his yelling only caused further unwanted attention.

John's antisocial behavior and Elly's misguided treatment of her son went on for years and caused him to cower in fear and become round-shouldered and tense. Most days, he had trouble figuring out how he was supposed to act or what type of boy he was supposed to be. He developed a poor self-image that affected him for many years.

Adding to his already dysfunctional childhood, John's older brother Ray persisted in teasing and tormenting him. Ray picked on his brother and never let John in on anything Ray was doing, causing John to feel insecure and unwanted by both his brother and his mother.

John became this skinny little kid with no sense of being anybody. He doubted his worth and whether he even had a place in the Kelly family. The young boy was destined to grow, of course, but graduated from eighth grade weighing only 102 pounds on a five-foot-two frame. Adding to his woes was a high, squeaky voice that his brother Ray and others made fun of at school.

᠉

Economic times were tough. John was born the year before the stock market crash in 1929 that led to the national depression lasting throughout his youth. The Great Depression years (1929-1933) meant the Kellys weren't always sure what they might eat for dinner.

John's father, Raymond, had grown up in Menlo Park, California and made it just through ninth grade at Bellarmine High School in College Park, San Jose. Once married to Elly, he traveled throughout California and Nevada selling mill supplies for Pacific Mills and Mines. He and one other salesman lasted on the job until 1933 when he joined his fellow 25 percent un-employed Americans as Pacific Mills folded like so many other Depression-ravaged companies. Raymond then picked up odd jobs digging ditches at Stanford University, setting up tents for shows at San Francisco Civic Auditorium, and selling tickets at nearby Kezar Stadium.

Both parents sacrificed for their sons. Elly baked and sold pies, secured a part-time bookkeeping job at a San Francisco canned goods company, and brought home unsaleable cans with missing labels. When desperate, the boys went down to the base-ment and shook the cans to guess the contents and decide what to have for dinner; many were fruit cocktail, some spaghetti, and some dog food, which they didn't eat.

Raymond was embarrassed by his loss of regular work. Elly had seen her Magnavox bookkeeping job and head bookkeeper opportunity slip away. Both troubled by uncertainty and food insecurity, they treaded water and did their best to raise John and his brothers. Dad Raymond was around more than he used to be, but mother Elly still ran the show at home.

~

By the mid-1930s, the Kelly family had rented a three-story San Francisco Victorian, but eventually the homeowner told Raymond the family had to buy or move. John's dad was not working regularly at the time, so panic had set in, but he and Elly talked the $3,750 asking price down to $3,250. Luckily, they were able to borrow $500 from a friend who had some PG&E stock, make the down payment, buy the house, and somehow scrape up their monthly payments. The roof leaked with buckets catching the drips. On Saturdays, John's dad climbed up on the roof to plug the holes with tar. Things were tough, but not des-perate, and the family managed like many others in their urban, mostly Irish Catholic San Francisco neighborhood.

John and his brothers Ray, Don, and Michael (born in 1937), grew up in the Haight Ashbury, now called Cole Valley, in San Francisco, a block from Golden Gate Park and Kezar Stadium. Without exception, the boys and their parents attended Sunday Mass. Once the church chore was completed, the youngsters played baseball and roamed the expansive park. Dad Raymond, a sports enthusiast, worked one of his part-time jobs at Kezar stadium taking tickets and selling football programs and often snuck the boys into games. Sometimes on weekends, the family traveled down the San Francisco Peninsula to Menlo Park to visit Elly's parents.

John later described his favorite grandmother, Elly's mother, Amania Jensen Poulsen, as one of "the most beautiful human beings I ever knew, warm and effusive." Elly's parents were once aristocratic and well-to-do, supported by her father Jens' large brick factory in Denmark. Apparently, his business partner had cheated him and he lost everything, which triggered the family's move to the United States.

Jens, supposedly a talented artist, once showed his art at an exhibition at a Paris fair, according to a family legend. Proud of two of Jens' paintings, John displayed them for years on his bedroom wall.

Of course, as new immigrants, Jens' family and social life had changed dramatically. No longer a factory owner, he became an hourly-wage house painter. Money was tight all around, and Elly's once wealthy folks were unable to offer financial help to her and her family. John later wondered if his mother's childhood had suffered due to her being the child of formerly wealthy Danish parents who made the European social scene. He questioned whether Elly received sufficient care and attention due to her parents' earlier busy, upper-class lifestyle.

Meanwhile, in the United States, the Great Depression ebbed gradually by the late thirties, but it took the World War II buildup effort to finally restore the United States economy and with it, the Kelly family. Raymond had the opportunity to gain regular good pay as a union asbestos worker. And incidentally, the Kellys were about to have one fewer mouth to feed.

TWO

Call to Be a Catholic Priest

S
T. AGNES GRAMMAR School nuns in San Francisco's
Haight Ashbury district had Kelly's vocation number,
which meant they thought him a prime prospect for the
priesthood. No wonder the nuns believed he had promise—Kelly
always helped them at school and served as an altar boy. These
nuns took pride in how many of their boy students entered the
seminary to study for priesthood. Early on, Kelly became the
designated future priest.

In spite of the nuns' expectations, Kelly experienced no vi-
sions, celestial appearances, or voices from above. Rather, in
the seventh grade, a visiting parish priest asked if any boys
had thought about becoming a priest. Recruiter priest Butch
Leonard, a former WWII Marine Corps Chaplain, made the case
for entering the priesthood. In the early 1940s, immediately following the Great Depression, four kids on Kelly's block entered
the seminary. They had all been encouraged by their dads, who

counseled that priesthood would mean a secure job, three square meals a day, and a roof over their heads.

Father Leonard wasn't pushy but told them to think about it. He asked if they had watched the priest in church and if that was something they might be inclined to do. As an altar boy, Kelly had been impressed, and after Father Leonard's talk, he couldn't get the priesthood idea out of his mind. This feeling lasted, and he felt a responsibility to investigate it, so he prayed for guidance from God regarding the possibility of that vocation. Looking for a sign, he often stopped after school at next-door St. Agnes' convent to hear Mexican nuns praying in chapel.

In eighth grade, entirely on his own, Kelly took the seminary entrance test and found out he passed but feared raising expectations, so he did not tell his parents. One of his eighth-grade classmates told his younger brother, Don, who rushed home and told their parents. Over the years, Kelly's relationship with his mother had turned a complete 180 degrees from her impossible problem child to her hope for the family, and she was pleased at the news.

Elly, in some ways, as noted, expected her boys to make up for her lack of career success. Less and less could she count on or control her oldest son Ray. So, despite her earlier frustrations and low expectations, the much-matured number-two Kelly son became her hope.

Catholic families in the late 1930s and early 1940s considered it a great honor to have a daughter become a nun or especially for a son to become a priest. Elly got wind of the nuns' encouragement and priestly expectations for Kelly, and things changed dramatically at home. Her attitude turned positive towards him, and he became the family ticket to parish prestige.

Kelly recognized his chance to be different from his brothers and to surpass problem-brother Ray and win Elly's love and approval. Despite those early difficulties and struggles with his domineering mother, he became her good boy "Jacky." Sadly, he won her short-term approval for his new potential priest role, but he would never feel her unconditional love.

Top-student Kelly graduated at thirteen years old and earned himself a scholarship to the highly-rated St. Ignatius High School in San Francisco. He turned it down and instead began his long road to the priesthood in September 1942. John felt strong faith evenly mixed with doubts. He wondered if he had truly been chosen by God to be a priest. To slip from the shadow of his older brother, to be the success his mother sought, and hopefully to please God, he entered the seminary.

Seminary Life for Young Kelly

As the twig is bent, so grows the tree, and in Kelly's youth, the Catholic Church recruited boys right out of the eighth grade, reasoning they would interest them before they discovered sex. Kelly for sure hadn't happened upon sex, but he still harbored misgivings about his vocation. Nevertheless, he committed to beginning the process of becoming a priest in the minor seminary.

Once accepted in September 1942, not yet a year after Pearl Harbor, Kelly entered the St. Joseph's College Minor Seminary in Mountain View, California. WWII was not yet going well, and the country's mood was fearful and uncertain. Kelly, along with fifty-five other pubescent high school freshmen, left home and arrived at St. Joseph's. Like many of his compatriots, he sought a safe harbor in the seminary.

St. Joseph's provided four years of high school and two years of college in a monastic environment. Kelly and fellow seminarians were detached from family except for visits from 1 to 4 p.m. on the third Sunday of every month, during summertime and during the two-week Christmas vacation. Parents were allowed entry only into the front parlor and on the flat land outside where they would have a picnic. At 4 p.m., the bell rang, parents departed, and the seminarians retreated into their domicile. Other than this visiting time, the boys saw no one from the outside. Elly wrote once a week, but that Sunday visit was his only contact with Raymond.

Furloughed for summer vacation, the seminarians were expected to attend Mass every day. Prior to leaving in June, each was assigned a research topic to present to their class when school began in fall. Also required was two or three weeks of summer community service such as acting as a camp counselor at a boys' camp or teaching catechism. One year, Kelly taught catechism at Saints Peter and Paul Parish in San Francisco's North Beach with, to quote Kelly himself, "three hundred screaming Italian kids." He also counseled at Pop Philips' boys' camp in Healdsburg, north of the big city.

Once the summer concluded, it was back to class. Kelly appreciated the camaraderie of his fifty-five St. Joseph's high school freshmen classmates but thought the academics only adequate with some good and some horrible teachers. He was labeled the "Greek Geek" since he loved Latin and Greek, subjects his classmates detested. They all used a cheat-sheet "pony" from an earlier class, while he translated from scratch. He once gave a speech on "The Value of Greek and Latin in the Minor Seminary." His classmates thought he was strange, but Kelly would teach Latin years later.

Seminary classes were Monday, Tuesday, Wednesday, Friday, and Saturday, and on those days, students could not converse at dinner; rather, they listened to readings and speeches from a pulpit. Occasionally, a visiting priest created a bit of excitement by sharing dinner with them and allowing them the honor of talking in his presence. Kelly confessed that sometimes on their own, they called up a priest to come visit so they would have a chance to talk. Students had Thursdays and Sundays off.

Each day after breakfast, the youngsters returned to their individual rooms only to make their beds. Much later, after study hall from 7:30 to 8:30 p.m., followed by night prayers, they were allowed back to their rooms for the "Great Silence." They were not to speak to anyone until breakfast the next morning. The rule was often broken by students talking to each other out of their windows. The common bathroom at the head of each stairway was locked at 10 p.m. each evening. If someone forgot to use the bathroom before lockdown, his tricky recourse was to pee out of the window into the shrubbery below.

Dorm rooms were single occupancy, and as the "fiercest rule of the seminary," anyone caught in another person's room was automatically expelled. Students were not allowed to socialize anywhere above the first common-area floor. School administration provided multiple social activities and helped vent their youthful male energies with sports.

When a boy arrived at the seminary, he was picked by the Ramblers, Trojans, or Bears, each multi-sport team captained by a sixth-year student. There were three levels of intramural competition, one for each two-year group, and they kept track of who won. The better players, including Kelly, also played semi-pro San Jose Orioles baseball on summer weekends. He usually occupied left outfield, but for a while, he was a left-handed third baseman.

As a minor seminary concession, the seminarians were permitted to walk to a local store and consume junk food and once per semester were authorized to walk to the town of Los Altos. For that outing, they had to sign up and be accompanied by a professor. They were forbidden to hitchhike, although some did and scrambled out of the car before being spotted by the professor on duty.

The lone regular woman on campus, except for an order of nuns from Canada who cooked the seminarians' meals, washed their clothes, and kept the kitchen clean, was the seminary nurse, Edna Bolling. The working nuns were not allowed to talk to students and typically prayed and hid in the kitchen—only nods in passing were allowed.

In addition to Edna and the nuns, Genevieve, a Mexican girl, worked for a while in the office store. Seminarians would go to there to buy pencils, make a subsequent trip to buy binder paper, and make yet another to buy other supplies. She lasted about six weeks before the faculty caught on to what the boys were doing and kicked her out. [Author's note: The sexist seminary approach has been described as an ugly deprivation of maturity, manhood, and adulthood. Richard Sipe, a famous U.S. psychologist who wrote about clerical celibacy, called priests "forever fourteen"— charging that young men in the seminary are not given a chance to develop.]

Kelly, never really challenged academically, easily cruised to graduate Maxima Cum Laude from St. Joseph. Largely sheltered and isolated from family and anxiety of war and postwar times, minor seminary life remained a peaceful and uncomplicated oasis. Unfortunately, seminary life kept Kelly trapped in state of male immaturity. Summer vacations continued his association with boys (his brothers and fellow seminarians), and a male priest led daily Mass. Being considered junior priests meant they were outside the realm of anything to do with girls or women. As he matured physically from thirteen to nineteen, he increasingly wondered what sex was about. He felt sheltered and clueless in his all-male bubble.

Upon finishing his education at St. Joseph, Kelly enrolled at St. Patrick's Seminary in Menlo Park, California for two additional years of college followed by four years of theology. There he earned a BA degree in philosophy with a minor in Latin. During this second six-year stretch, continuing classmate Tom

McMahon described Kelly as "smarter than some of the professors." McMahon claimed that, in Greek studies, Kelly never made a mistake and that he had little regard for the intelligence level of the faculty.

At this more senior level, seminarians still had to conform without question to the system, to the rules of dress, to the intellectual approach to studies, and to virtuous behavior both on and off campus. They only vaguely realized they were constantly being watched during all twelve years to see if they would be obedient. Anyone who couldn't or didn't follow the rules was dismissed.

Kelly and McMahon, however, broke a number of rules without getting caught, including purchasing a $200 sailboat they kept at nearby Redwood City Harbor. Very cautiously, they hid the buying and sailing of the boat and were never caught. Classmates never suspected their disobedience because of a culture of separation and secrecy, which typically prevented fellow seminarians from knowing much about each other.

The practice involved each seminarian being blended in the beginning into the category of minor seminarian and further blending into the pre-priest category at St. Patrick's Seminary, which is all in preparation for the ultimate immersion into the priesthood as an anonymous person. Each seminarian would become a priest (ultimately, a pastor) and would be transferred to a different parish from time to time. The continuing advice was therefore, "Don't make many friends; just do the job, be obedient, and stay away from women."

The seminary mission was to make monks of the seminarians yet expect them to later live in the real world of priesthood as part of a secular society. Kelly blended and conformed just enough to make it through his twelve pre-priest seminary years, but remnants of his individuality survived and lay dormant, destined to reappear years later.

Kelly's first six years at St. Joseph left him totally clueless about sexual matters, and he had no knowledge of the details of intercourse until years later. The St. Patrick's years then became increasingly difficult due to his ignorance and confused sexual feelings and the contrary and unnatural rules of the Church. He felt that something was wrong with him. The Church taught or implied that priests were to reach a state so holy that they were beyond sexual feelings. Just having forbidden thoughts was considered sinful.

From time to time, Kelly wondered how he could be having banned sexual feelings yet imagine becoming a holy priest. He feared he would not, or could not, meet lofty spiritual expectations of the Holy Mother Church and attain the venerated office of priesthood. He struggled to push his doubts aside and pressed on to honor his original commitment to become a priest.

Kelly Becomes a Priest

Catholic Holy Orders are a series of steps that lead to becoming a priest. Kelly's vocational commitment began at the end of the second year of St. Patrick's Major Seminary with the ceremony of tonsure. Sub-deacon came at the end of the fourth year, deacon at the end of the fifth year, and priest at the end of the sixth year.

Gnawing doubts delayed Kelly's sub-deacon ceremony as he came to grips with the impending vow of celibacy. On the day of the service, his commitment wavered. He panicked, left the altar, and absented himself for a time. He didn't have the urge to have sex or be married; he just felt confused about sexuality. He wanted to feel better inside but ultimately decided, in any case, to honor his commitment to become a priest. He returned after a bit and became a sub-deacon.

Kelly continued his studies at St. Patrick's and looked with trepidation toward his final commitment, the sacrament and ceremony of ordination. Little did he know, he was about to learn of an unpleasant financial surprise that would add to his fears.

Just a week before his ordination as a priest, the seminary treasurer called Kelly into his office and asked him how he would pay back all the tuition that he was unable to pay during twelve seminary years. It boggled Kelly's mind that the Church considered tuition and expenses his personal debt. The Church's solution was for Kelly and other poor seminarians to take out a fifteen-year life insurance policy so that if they died, the seminary and the archdiocese would recover their investment.

Kelly had ridden out WWII in minor seminary, and the Korean War started and ended while he was in major seminary. Although insulated from wars and their accompanying economic and social changes, he continued to feel as uncertain as the world around him. That fateful Friday, June 11, 1954, after twelve years of singular focus, study, and devotion, he struggled to overcome nagging doubts about his pending final commitment to life as a priest.

Even prostrate on the altar, dressed in a simple white cassock, Kelly whispered to the seminarian to his right, asking him to stop Kelly if he tried to leave. Despite his fear and anxious state of mind, he soldiered ahead and was ordained as a priest with a cohort of thirty-five others at Old St. Mary's Cathedral in San Francisco.

After ordination, the somewhat relieved Kelly and his proud folks celebrated at a Fisherman's Wharf diner. The very next Sunday, he said his first Mass, a defining moment in his life, and afterwards attended a reception for family and friends. At the end of that party, Kelly, somewhat sheepishly, gave everybody a blessing. He wondered how that symbolic, ritualistic consecration as a priest gave him a power to give other, perhaps holier human beings a blessing as if from God. The notion didn't sit well with him, nor did what he learned next.

The celebration had barely ended when Kelly received a taste of church politics and observed the preferential treatment of two fellow classmate brothers from a wealthy Peninsula family. Immediately upon becoming priests, both were sent to major cities, one to Oakland and one to San Francisco, where they would have many opportunities for lucrative pay-to-pray Mass stipends—typically cash in an envelope after the service.

Catholics believe in purgatory for those who die and aren't quite "good enough" to go directly to heaven. To rescue departed relatives who may be interim residents of this stopover, they believe that a Mass said in those suffering souls' honor would quicken their release to heaven. Traditionally, during these and other church ceremonies, an offering is made to the celebrant priest, who is usually permitted to keep it for himself since parish priests do not take a vow of poverty.

Wealthy, older big-city parishes typically scored substantial stipends for resident priests. But poor-family, tuition-deficient Kelly was assigned to St. Eugene's Parish in a small Santa Rosa community (north of San Francisco in the rural country) where few older, wealthier people lived and where he could expect virtually no Mass stipends. Martin Luther had, many years earlier, effectively ended the practice of paid indulgences, but he had failed to strangle the Catholic Mass stipend practice.

Although Church favoritism to wealthy families upset him, Kelly's lack of stipend spending money was not burdensome to him since he never had much, either at home or during his time at the seminary. Kelly's most challenging adjustment was social, not financial, as he would now have to deal with women and with other regular people. As noted, he had had no experience with sex, presumably other than masturbation, and yet was expected to counsel married couples. After preaching total abstinence to unmarried folk, he now had to advise newly married couples, as he understood it, that "any part of your body can touch any part of your partner's." Kelly knew he was way out of his depth counseling couples since his social background had been almost all male, all the time.

Until his Santa Rosa parish assignment, it had been all about male companionship—male classmates in the seminary taught by male priests and instructors, all with little understanding of and no interaction with girls. He had been told and retold that as seminarians studying to be priests, they were "special." If they committed a sexual act, it wouldn't be just a mortal sin—it would be a sacrilege, because they were sacred. Thus, Kelly had negative thoughts about sex, regarding it as taboo.

Seminary instructors had preached that there were different vocations in life—marriage or priesthood—and that seminarians, as future priests, were "way above everybody else." A series of books on religion in high school minor seminary had included two pages about sexuality. Kelly's teacher had told the students not to read those pages and to staple them together. They were also not permitted to own an Old Testament Bible because there were "sex stories" in it. Kelly was deliberately kept clueless, and all through seminary, over and over, he was taught to have nothing to do with women and that they would land him in trouble.

Gender segregation continued after ordination. All recreation took place with Kelly's fellow male priests—golf on Wednesday and golf vacations to Monterey or Santa Cruz with three or four other priests. Kelly saw this strange denial of anything sexual as an elephant in the room.

The anti-sex, anti-female message stuck. Kelly never knew how to relate to women—he was not hateful, but never completely trusting of them. Externally, he appeared comfortable with women, but internally he felt challenged by their presence throughout his life. In groups he had been involved in, he perceived some women as "dominant and controlling in a sneaky, aggressive way." Kelly generally avoided women, but they found him handsome and they did not avoid him, and his superiors recognized early on that young girls were attracted to Kelly.

One of the priest's duties at St. Eugene's was to serve as chaplain to the nearby Los Guilicos juvenile detention facility, which assisted troubled teenage girls from around the state. Church administrators recognized immediately that the handsome Kelly was a tempting distraction for the incarcerated young girls, and the administrators promptly shipped him off to St. Emydius' (patron saint for protection against earthquakes) parish in San Francisco before any trouble could occur.

This San Francisco Ingleside neighborhood rectory had a pastor and two assistants. As the youngest priest assistant, Kelly oversaw parish teenagers and younger children, including a teen club and all kinds of activities like CYO (Catholic Youth Organization).

The eighty-year-old Irish pastor, Father Motherway, liked Kelly, but as number three in the pecking order, Kelly was forced to learn obedience. Although Kelly thought they were friends, the pastor would become upset with him for seemingly trivial things—once for overfilling incense with the wrong hand and once, more significantly, for sticking the pastor with an afternoon baptism while Kelly, without notice or permission, snuck out for a San Francisco Forty-Niners football game.

Initially, Kelly enjoyed his new assignment at St. Emydius' because he spent his time there mostly with children. He opened the gym on Sunday afternoon to play with kindergarteners through eighth-graders. Still, as a young, newly minted cleric, Kelly felt presumptuous blessing and advising families and his more mature congregation from the pulpit. He couldn't reconcile being twenty-six years old and telling much more experienced people how to live their lives. He struggled with how he could advise them and counsel on spiritual matters while he struggled with his own spirituality and commitment. In spite of his growing doubts, Kelly liked and appreciated the parishioners and had a good deal of fun with them.

By the end of his second year at St. Emydius, however, Kelly had grown to seriously doubt his fitness for the duties and rituals of parish life. He had reached the point where he no longer felt like saying Sunday Mass or that he even fit the role of priest. He would convince a visiting priest to say his assigned Mass while Kelly took off for the nearby Pacific Ocean shoreline where he would just sit and gaze at the calming waves.

As Kelly's internal conflict and confusion became more intense, he began to think about leaving the priesthood. In the summer of 1956, just two years after ordination, he wrote a letter to his parents telling them that he would be leaving the Church to hide out in Canada and that he just had to leave. He kept the letter for a long time, but never mailed it. Providence or luck intervened.

In yet another defining moment in his life, Kelly received notice of his transfer to Junípero Serra High School in San Mateo, a Catholic boys' school south of San Francisco. When asked about teaching earlier by the those in charge of assignments, he had declined those duties. In the interim, however, Kelly had become intrigued about working with young people and decided to at least consider what Serra had to offer.

He never regretted that decision.

THREE

Serra High School

DESPITE HIS CONTINUED misgivings about his vocation as a priest, John Kelly arrived at all-male Serra High School in San Mateo, California where he discovered he would be living in a faculty house with twelve priests. After his two-year stint at family-friendly St. Emydius' Parish in San Francisco, he returned to a world where women were absent.

After twelve years of all-male seminary followed by an all-male high school, Kelly still had little opportunity to learn to deal with women and seemed destined to forever struggle with those relationships. At this time, a woman would not even be considered for faculty at Serra High School. As Kelly recalled later, "She'd be looked upon with scorn if she even tried to be involved."

Much to his surprise, the high school environment suited Kelly. Serra fit him perfectly since he no longer had to worry about the official things he had to do as a parish priest. He was

able to interact daily with students, whom he came to love dearly, and he soon saw his assignment "not as work but really as fun, sheer joy." He lost his desire to renounce priesthood and abandoned thoughts of escaping to Canada. At Serra, he had a chance to exercise some limited individuality and experiment with his own ideas of spirituality.

For example, his dissatisfaction with official church services led him to create an approach somewhat different from established ritual. As athletic team chaplain, whenever Serra had a football game, he would say a Mass at 9 a.m., and then preach an "out-of-the-norm sermon to get the kids involved." Afterwards, they would all go out to breakfast. He wasn't as closely supervised at the high school as he had been before, and he found he had much more freedom than at his earlier parish assignment in San Francisco.

Carl "Red" Moroney was part of Kelly's first-year 1956 freshman homeroom class and had Kelly for a counselor. At age twenty-eight, Kelly was not that much older than Moroney or his fellow students and, as Kelly recalled, was "as apprehensive as they were on the first day of high school."

Moroney remembered that Kelly was really into kids and sports—his students even gave him the nickname "Jock." Kelly's relationship with the students was special for him since he had never experienced regular high school, having gone to seminary right out of grade school.

Without official sanction, Father Jock would drive the kids to ball games, take them on overnight trips, and do other things a teacher could never do in the present day. Like a big kid himself, Kelly would pile five or six boys into his old black Plymouth sedan and take them to various events, including a Los Angeles track meet. As freshman basketball coach, he often transported many of the players to their games.

During the first year at Serra, Kelly realized he needed to replace the sedan with a station wagon so he could accommodate and haul more students around. Even though cigarette smoke drove him crazy, and he tried to convince the boys not to smoke, he still let them smoke in the car. If his superior had found out, he would have been in trouble at Serra, but he laughed about it later in life.

Moroney told this author that one weekend, Father Jock gathered a bunch of the students to rake, drag, and line the baseball field for the upcoming year's games. Moroney said, "Kelly made it seem like volunteering, but more likely we were in some sort of trouble and this was part of the discipline."

To assist the effort, Kelly had borrowed a large truck and loaded the necessary work tools to bring to the field. Moroney was standing up in the back of the truck, and just as Kelly turned into the school driveway, a connecting overhead archway caught Moroney right in the head and knocked him out cold.

Kelly tended to the injured Moroney, but he was afraid that he had stretched the rules too much this time and was concerned about potential administrative consequences. He could have been fired and even sued by Moroney's parents if his scheme had been uncovered, but that didn't happen. Moroney remained Kelly's friend for many years after the incident, but never let him forget that the big scar on his hairline was a result of Kelly's work crew misadventure.

Despite his sometimes unorthodox behavior, Kelly was considered an excellent and rigorous teacher, recognized for his knowledge of Latin and Greek. In the "jug," i.e. after-school detention in the library, Kelly made the fifty or so detained students write Latin for the entire hour.

During one school semester, Moroney ignored Kelly for a while over what Moroney thought was an unfair grade. Later, after a football practice, Kelly grabbed and pulled him into a side room, told him he was tired of his attitude, and punched the student lightly on the chest, scaring him. Instead of reporting the incident, Moroney said he straightened out and "stopped acting like a jerk."

Kelly acknowledged that he was strict. When he became Dean of Students, he enforced a dress code: no jeans, only shirts with a collar, leather shoes—no Keds or sandals. He often sent improperly dressed kids home to change and then put them in detention after school.

The rules applied to all school functions, even weekend football and basketball games, where Kelly carried a pocket notebook and scribbled in offenders' names. On Monday mornings, he announced on the PA those students required to report to detention. He leaned especially hard on freshmen and sophomores.

The job became easier for the upperclassmen since "the fear was already in place"—fear of Kelly for his tough standards, that is. By the time the previous disturbers and troublemakers became seniors, they knew how to stay in his good graces, and they would buddy up to Kelly on the school yard.

Dolores Kelly-Hons and Al Hons had four boys who were students at Serra. Dolores called Kelly "very strict." She was terrified when she had to call Father Kelly to say one of her boys was sick and couldn't attend school, fearing she would be seen as coddling her son.

Kelly's philosophy was to make sure students knew that he was in charge, yet to act as a human being so they would understand that he was also their friend. He enforced school regulations, but also drove students around town during leisure hours. He felt successful on the discipline side when once he looked up at the auditorium ceiling and saw "F____ Kelly" scrawled there. Kelly treated teenagers as young people who had their own agendas and were a lot of fun but who needed guidance and discipline. The boys generally appreciated Kelly's approach.

Kelly maintained that teens at Serra were like cats when you first met them—they wanted to know who you were and what were you doing there. But after they got to know you, they were like dogs and wanted to be petted and shown attention. He said later there was "not a single day that I did not enjoy walking into the Serra High School building."

John Horgan, also a Serra freshman during Kelly's first year, later a well-known local newspaper reporter, told this author that Serra had some stellar individual athletes and that Kelly nurtured those young men. The Catholic school was just starting to flex its athletic program muscles as enrollment grew and its teams and their reputations became stronger. Kelly loved it when the Serra football, basketball, and baseball teams defeated their archrival, Jesuit Bellarmine Prep of San Jose.

John Barrett, Serra Class of '69, described Kelly as "tough but helpful. No nonsense old school. The big fist." Barrett told this author he generally avoided teachers, especially Kelly, but later realized that Kelly had helped him become a better person.

Regarding Kelly's athletic prowess, Gerry Bundy, another Serra student at the time, told this author that Kelly had a good hook shot, which he often demonstrated during Senior/Faculty basketball games. His advantage was thought to be a bent pinky finger, which Kelly attributed to a diving endzone touchdown score during a touch football game at St. Patrick's Seminary.

NOTRE DAME UNIVERSITY AND THE SEGREGATED SOUTH

In September 1967, peace and quiet prevailed at the almost lily-white suburban Serra region of the San Francisco Peninsula while the "Summer of Love" wound down in the city's Haight Ashbury. But Newark, New Jersey, and Detroit were cleaning up after the deadly "long, hot summer" race riots, and college campus protests were increasing as Vietnam War military casualties reached their peak.

During this time, the San Francisco Catholic Archdiocese chose to send thirty-eight-year-old Kelly to Notre Dame University in South Bend, Indiana to advance his study of theology. As much as he had enjoyed teaching, he felt the general pressure of his Serra day-to-day classroom work, and increasingly, he felt distressed by the deteriorating social conditions in the unsettled nation. He figured that a sabbatical would let him just be a student and allow him to "hang loose" with no duties as a priest or teacher. The antiwar protests and other civil unrest had not taken hold at Notre Dame yet, so he focused on his religious studies.

Kelly began to discover information about the 1940s and '50s theological world, including surprising new concepts purposefully not introduced in the old-school seminary where old-world religious views were a staple. He was amazed to learn about modern interpretations of scripture—the notion that the Bible was open to interpretation according to the culture in which it was written.

Ever curious, Kelly learned that beginning in the 1950s, theological and biblical studies in the Catholic Church trended away from earlier literal interpretations of the Bible. Catholic theology then began to integrate modern human experience with Church principles based on the teachings of Jesus. This approach suited Kelly who, for the first time, began to see a world that was not so black and white. He realized that "the God force in this world and within the Church was developing in a spirit of openness to new things, to growth, and even to other religions and forms of faith. Ecumenism was in the air."

Pope John the 23rd's Second Vatican Council had begun in 1962 and ended December 1965, just two years before Kelly had arrived at Notre Dame. Dramatic Catholic Church change followed the council. Latin aficionado Kelly found some changes disturbing, like the now widespread use of vernacular languages such as English in the Mass instead of traditional Latin. Yet he cheered on the embryonic move away from pointy hats and lace clerical regalia worn by cardinals and bishops, whose stature was now reduced a peg or two.

One change Father Kelly particularly liked, given his outgoing personality, was the directive to celebrate the Mass facing outward instead of facing the altar with his back to the congregation. Kelly was quick to endorse the council's aesthetic changes, which affected and modernized Catholic liturgical music and artwork. The less formal guitar folk Mass was beginning to replace the Latin choir hymns of the traditional Mass.

Ensconced in an academic environment of active liberal ideas at Notre Dame, Kelly concluded that the human race had the world entrusted to it so that, as he once said, "you don't sit still with it, rather you keep learning new things because new things are discovered all the time." His belief was reinforced that there was no conflict between science and theology, contrary to the fundamentalist anti-evolution he had been taught in the seminary. Increasingly, he saw science as "a gift of God to learn more and more about this world." "At Notre Dame," he reported later, "my whole thinking began to change dramatically." Kelly's thinking was about to receive a further jolt, this time around the issues of racial and social justice.

January academic exams had just been successfully completed, and upon returning from a semester break, Kelly learned of an opportunity to pursue his evolving interest in social justice—in this case, the civil rights movement in the South. He had stayed in touch with five or six Serra High School graduates, now students at Notre Dame, including Dan Johndrow. He asked Kelly if he would be willing to travel with a college student group to South Carolina during the upcoming Easter vacation break to register Black voters. At the end of January, Kelly, Johndrow, and Kelly's roommate Kevin Kentfield, along with more than a dozen Notre Dame students, signed up and committed to the trip scheduled for the middle of April 1968.

It was unsettling, even dangerous, in the South. On the first day of February, the day after Kelly and his crew signed up to travel to South Carolina, two Black Memphis sanitation workers were killed in the line of duty leading to an extended union strike. On February 8, three Black students were shot to death by highway patrol officers at the Orangeburg Massacre at South Carolina State University. Kelly and Johndrow discussed the increasing danger but decided they would honor their commitment and make the trip.

On April 4, 1968, Martin Luther King Jr. was assassinated in Memphis, an event which was followed by four days of rioting and protests in 110 cities around the country. Kelly and Johndrow, this time more seriously, questioned the wisdom of a venture into the volatile South. They decided once again to honor their commitment and departed from the South Bend, Indiana university campus on April 9, the evening of King's funeral in Atlanta. By caravan with four other carloads of students, they drove throughout the night and approached Hampton, South Carolina at about 10 a.m. on Wednesday, April 10. Nearing the town proper, they passed rows of "welcome" committee pickup trucks lining both sides of the two-lane road. In the rear of the trucks, having been warned of the approach of "outside white agitators," waited more than a dozen KKK men, each armed with a menacing shotgun intended to intimidate Kelly and the arriving young male and female students.

Uneasy but undeterred, the group continued on to the Hampton County headquarters of the head of the National Association for the Advancement of Colored People (NAACP). There they met their host and settled into their bunks. The NAACP had lined up a crew of Black youngsters about the ages of the students to join their group and drive the white Notre Dame volunteers around to Black neighborhoods to register people to vote. The county population at that time was 90 percent Black but governed by the 10 percent minority whites.

Kelly immediately hit it off and became great friends with two of the volunteers, Fast Eddie and Easy Eddie, who were about eighteen or nineteen years old. Later, he recalled, "They were two of the nicest kids I had ever met," and he regretted not having stayed in touch with them. They drove Kelly and Johndrow around as their team went door to door and asked folks to register, mostly without difficulty. Kelly remembered that the Black neighborhoods were very neat and well-kept but very isolated. The group of volunteers were shadowed and watched wherever they went by men following them in one of those "welcome" pickup trucks.

At one point, Kelly's team decided to stop and grab a drink and something to eat. The local youngsters left the car with Kelly and walked into a café. The other customers there all froze; they seemed stunned to see a white adult and students associating with two Black youngsters. Kelly recalled, "They were shocked this was happening, but there was no trouble."

The voter registration location was five or six miles from where they were staying, and as Kelly drove back one night, a South Carolina Highway Patrolman followed him closely the entire way. He seemed to be waiting for Kelly to make a mistake, but he didn't, and no incident occurred. One of the Notre Dame students was stopped by the police and received a ticket. They decided to appeal and found a white judge who was holding court in the backyard of his house. Kelly recalled, "They all thought the hearing was a farce," causing the ticket to stand.

On Easter Sunday morning, the NAACP leader invited Kelly to say Catholic Mass in the man's front yard before a congregation of the students and about twenty-five Black locals. Kelly later said he "was embarrassed forever that I didn't invite the Black people to receive Communion because I was still hung up on Catholic rules."

The college volunteers were invited afterwards to participate in a Baptist church service out in the countryside where, at the invitation of the preacher, Kelly added his sermon. Kelly advised the Black congregants, "If you are ever finally liberated and treated equally in society, do not change your beautiful togetherness—maintain your close family ties." He recalled that, for the first time, he watched a congregation raise their arms saying,

"Yay, yay!" to his remarks. Dan Johndrow reported that then, after a twenty-minute social, the preacher and Kelly performed a joint bread and wine Eucharistic meal service. The two clerics were joined at a long temporary table by all the participants.

Monday night, April 15, before the team returned Tuesday to Notre Dame, the Black residents hosted an appreciation party in their little hall outside of town. There, Kelly recalled with a smile, the white students from Notre Dame "danced up a storm with the South Carolina Black girls and boys and that probably hadn't happened before." Johndrow said the event was "a once-in-a-lifetime experience," and to the amusement of the Black youth, he and the white students "found rhythm and dance moves they never knew they had."

This South Carolina Black voter registration experience was Kelly's first real encounter with Black culture, and it powerfully and permanently imprinted on him a love and respect. He began to realize the scope of their challenges, having seen firsthand the deeply ingrained racial bias and lack of social justice for an entire race of American citizens. Kelly's courageous trip to register southern Black voters awakened him to their plight and inspired his lifelong dedication to helping minorities, especially Black youth and adult males.

Weeks later, back on the Notre Dame campus, Kelly was asked to substitute at Mass for the pastor of a white parish in a minority Black neighborhood in South Bend. When he asked the pastor how he helped those nearby Black minorities, he was disappointed to hear, "It is none of our business—they aren't Catholic." Kelly held the contrary point of view that the whole purpose of being a Christian was to make a real difference, both locally and globally.

Kelly's time at Notre Dame cemented his realization that "you need to be true to yourself and be sure what you are thinking, saying, and doing fits with who you are." Increasingly, he could see that the social issues concerning him could not be undertaken given his current status as a priest—the Catholic Church's organizational structure would not accommodate his desire to focus on racial and social justice issues.

In a true blessing, the Notre Dame experience had provided Kelly a taste of liberation theology, and Vatican II had shown him a way of spiritual renewal for the Church. In studying contemporary theology, he had learned not to take the Bible literally but rather to see it as a collection of stories meant to teach a point. The point or the lesson was important, not the literal language.

Kelly had discovered from a modern Catholic university the chasm between the fundamentalist, ritualistic Catholic Church of his experience and the simple Bible lessons of compassion and love. These newfound ideas, especially his adventurous deep-south Black voter registration drive, changed Kelly forever.

The Notre Dame experience had added fuel to his dissatisfaction with Church bureaucracy and empty ritual. A social justice fire was igniting in Kelly's belly, and he began wondering again about his vocation as a priest and his long-term career path.

CAREER DOUBTS

John Kelly returned home from his Notre Dame sabbatical in June 1968, just months after the Vietnam Tet Offensive and the long-building and now galvanizing public disenchantment with the war. Back at Serra with an expanded perspective and new awareness, he was receptive and sympathetic to a subculture of similarly disillusioned young men. He connected and "felt really at ease with them and promoted their cause." He began his renegade transformation.

Shortly after his return to San Mateo, the area deanery (a San Francisco Archdiocese subregion) invited him to debrief his fellow priests about his Notre Dame experience. Kelly obliged and relayed thoughts and ideas about contemporary theology. No sooner had he finished than the head of the deanery told him and the group that this was "all very nice but had nothing to do with the Catholic Church."

To his dismay, Kelly's message there and generally among his fellow priests was not appreciated and had little lasting effect. He continued to see the Catholic Church as stuck and "hung-up by tradition and image." The old liturgy and catechism were not dealing with the real world. As he said at the time, "the Church wasn't progressing from the old to the new."

At Serra, Kelly now felt conflicted. He wanted to be sure that he was teaching, speaking, and practicing this new truth. He believed he should bring along parts of the old religion that still fit, yet change and discard the traditional Church doctrine that no longer applied to modern life. Initially assigned to teach three traditional religion classes at Serra, Kelly balked. He told the understanding principal that he couldn't do it, that he no longer fit into that program, and he was granted a leave of absence. Still in residence, he instead spent more and more time outside of class "to help kids get engaged" with local and world events and their place in society.

Kelly increasingly became aware that the Church didn't worry about racial integration because there were few minorities attending Catholic schools. Wealthier, generally white San Francisco Peninsula parents predominantly sent their Catholic children to private or Catholic schools.

During this time, the national battle to break down racial barriers had become fierce. In response to King's murder and the subsequent riots, President Lyndon Johnson signed The Fair Housing Act into law on April 11, 1968. It began the long national challenge of preventing housing discrimination based on race, sex, national origin, and religion.

Kelly knew that only a very few Black youngsters attended Serra. He became friends with some of them and learned several reasons why they came to the nearly all-white Serra. One was because some of their families just wanted their kids to obtain a better education. These minority youngsters had not been raised Catholic, though the other students at Serra accepted them readily. The Black kids left after school and went back into their home culture, which was a different world from the local white neighborhoods.

Lynn Swann, later the star NFL pro football player, was not Catholic but became a highly respected Black student leader at Serra due to his great deal of talent. Billy Jackson, another Black student, was asked as senior in 1971 what it was like to be at that school. He recalled, "During the day I'm here and it is fine with the guys. When we go home everybody else goes west and I go east," referencing the fact that that on the San Francisco Peninsula the predominately white wealthy areas were west, and the generally poor Black and Latino areas were east.

As time passed, Kelly upped his involvement in race and integration issues, which he believed the Church was neglecting. He joined the local Conference on Religion, Race, and Social Concern, which then became the Interfaith Network for Community Health (INCH). This ecumenical community group dealt specifically with integration issues. Kelly began to meet with them every Wednesday morning at the African Methodist Episcopal (A.M.E.) Zion Church in San Mateo. The group included the Black pastor at A.M.E., the pastor from Catholic St. Gregory's, a representative from the Protestant Church, and Rabbi Sanford Rosen of San Mateo Peninsula Temple Beth El.

Kelly later said that at the time, he increasingly recognized "a gap between what I thought Jesus was all about, what he expected us to do in the world, and what the Catholic Church actually did in my own community." He attended a local Thanksgiving conference that included people from all Christian denominations and other religions as well. A main topic of this event was the historic late-1960s integration of the schools. However, some Christian religious communities refused to participate because funds from a conference collection were targeted for non-Christian charitable causes.

While at Serra, Kelly had many friends and influenced hundreds of young folks, but the challenge of teaching boys and participating in all manner of sports ultimately was not enough for him. More and more, his interests and passions were becoming local and national social issues, especially racial integration. He felt a call to action—to make a difference in the world.

In 1969, several parishioners were up in arms about nearby St. Matthew's Grammar School, having decided to hold their eighth-grade picnic at the still-segregated San Mateo Elks Club. Several angered parents of those students pleaded their issue to St. Matthew's school principal but were unable to have the venue changed. The parents then tried the parish pastor and finally went to the governing archdiocese, but they were unsuccessful; no one would touch the hot-button issue. The venue remained the segregated Elks Club.

Shortly thereafter, a Serra freshman student with a white mother and a Black father snuck fliers into the Serra faculty mailboxes, inviting them to the nearby King Community Center for a meeting that evening to discuss the St. Matthews picnic. The Serra principal learned what was happening and harshly told the student that a St. Matthew's event was none of the Serra school's business and to take his fliers and leave the school immediately.

Kelly heard about the issue and how this student was treated and was furious. He spent the rest of the afternoon struggling with whether to go to the meeting at King Community Center. Finally, he decided to attend.

The group in attendance elected to picket St. Matthew's Church the following Sunday during the morning Masses. All day that Saturday, Kelly wondered again whether he ought to participate in the picketing. Finally, he told this author, "I realized, I had to say two Sunday morning Masses at another parish, so I couldn't go, so I said the hell with it."

But following his early Masses, Kelly's curiosity won out, and he drove to St. Matthew's, still debating whether he should or shouldn't now join the still active protest. A couple of those who had been at the King Center meeting saw Kelly, so he figured he was stuck and got out of his car. There he stood in his Roman collar at St. Matthew's Catholic Church, picketing the scheduled eighth-grade picnic at the segregated Elks Club. Many Catholic parents who had children at Serra and who belonged to the Elks Club were unhappy about seeing the protesting priest Kelly. [Author's note: Until 1973, the national constitution of the Elk lodge restricted membership to white men and did not admit women until 1998.]

Many white parents who saw Kelly were initially pleased to see him, but, when they realized why he was there, changed facial expressions dramatically. One father drove up with all his children and flipped Kelly the bird.

The St. Matthew's protest weekend began in earnest with Kelly's inner battle to protect his clerical public image and yet be honest and fair to his conscience. He hadn't needed to join the protest and could have taken the easy way out, but he thought the Church position was outlandishly wrong and had to be challenged. He was surprised that once he joined the protest, he felt relieved and no longer felt conflicted.

Father Tom McMahon, a friend of Kelly's, said that after he saw Kelly in clerical garb being harassed by a parishioner for protecting the Black students, Kelly was never the same, and his whole attitude toward the Church changed. He was correct, since Kelly thought it a shame that parents even had to protest to change the racially tone-deaf attitude of the Catholic Church.

Soon after his picketing trauma, the disgruntled, forty-year-old Kelly left the Serra faculty house and took up residence at St.

Mark's Church in Belmont while continuing to teach at Serra until the summer of 1972. His initial joy and satisfaction of teaching there was slipping away. He realized that his vocation as a Catholic priest might soon come to an end.

Another Straw Overloads the Camel

Up until the late 1960s, the Catholic school system functioned through the hiring of nuns, brothers, and priests as faculty with students' tuition only fifty dollars a month. Accordingly, the thirty Serra staff priests were not paid adequately; they were cheap labor with what Kelly labeled only "a pseudo salary and room and board." That salary never topped more than $100 a month with occasional Mass stipends.

Times changed, and with fewer clergy around, school administrators needed more and more lay people (called "lay helpers" by the superintendents) to maintain the Catholic schools. Most came right out of college, worked as practice teachers, and left for better paying public school jobs.

During the mid-1960s, the archdiocese developed a lay teacher contract and set a salary scale based upon public school salaries. By the late 1960s, when the contracts came up for renewal, the archdiocese balked at keeping public school salary parity because the public school salaries were increasing. Lay teachers at Serra and other Catholic schools decided the contract salary offers were unfair, and when negotiations failed, they voted to strike during the fall of 1971.

Throughout the diocese, only a few clergy, including Kelly, now residing at St. Mark's, went out on strike with a few younger Serra lay teachers. Oldest in service of the few priests there to strike, the archdiocese labeled him the ringleader. A former Serra priest, promoted to the archdiocese, called Kelly and said, "Okay, you've had your fun. Now get back to work." Kelly was taken aback by the comment and hung up on him.

Kelly observed that though the Catholic Church hierarchy proclaimed beautiful things about social justice, they did not practice what they preached, and they weren't always forthright. During the strike, the principal at Serra asked if the striking priests would like to meet with parents to explain their position. The priests agreed, but on the night the parents and priests met, the principal announced a last-minute priest gag order. A supporter in the audience said he wanted to hear what the priests and Father Kelly had to say.

Kelly rose to speak, but before he could speak several words, another parent stood up and yelled, "Who do you think you are? You are supposed to teach our kids. Go back to work. What do you think this is?" Kelly was silenced and walked out after the meeting ended. He encountered four ladies, formerly friends, who cornered and screamed at him for "ruining their kids' education and not doing his duty."

Upset with the way the Church authorities were handling the strike, Kelly wound up in this maelstrom for six weeks until the strike was settled. He never regretted his participation. He felt the archdiocese position was wrong and told friends, "I don't care who likes it or doesn't like it. I've got to say what I feel is right."

Kelly had disobeyed by challenging his fellow teachers and superiors. He incurred the wrath of parents, peers, and parishioners at a personal cost, but that was easy to bear because the students were on his side. After the assembly where Kelly was prevented from explaining his view, Serra students he met with at St. Mark's parish told him they were totally committed to the purpose of the strike.

The teachers, standing up for what they believed, succeeded in reaching a settlement, and the result of the strike was a fair benefit package and tenure. The archdiocese additionally developed a council of teachers who addressed the administration's issues, and the school developed an advisory parent group. The archdiocese finally realized that Serra and its other schools were going to be run by lay people and that if they wanted quality teachers, they had to pay them well and treat them well. [Author's note: In 2020, Serra High School had all lay teachers, only a part-time chaplain, and no faculty priests.]

Though the teachers had succeeded, the turmoil of the strike had spurred Kelly to consider leaving Serra completely. He knew if he continued to be a priest, he would become even more outspoken about social justice issues. That would not sit well with his Catholic superiors.

In late spring 1972, Serra convened a faculty meeting that was supposed to be a mini-celebration to mark the end of the schoolyear. But there was never any real harmony after the Serra strike; the opposing sides never came together again. Kelly realized he was a priest outside the clerical norm. He was proud to have joined the strike and knew that it was the right thing to do. Further, he knew that he no longer belonged at the school.

KELLY LEAVES SERRA HIGH SCHOOL

Still, the decision to leave was painful. Departing Serra High School felt like "leaving a womb," Kelly said later. He continued to live and handle parish duties at St. Mark's in Belmont until at age forty-four, in fall of 1973, he crossed the Bay to study at the Graduate Theological Union (GTU) in Berkeley for a year.

There, Kelly roomed for six months in the city of Pinole with a pastor who was also a fellow student, then moved to an apartment in the nearby city of Concord. In June 1974, Kelly graduated with a master's degree in psychology. The Church paid his tuition. He greatly appreciated that as well as his opportunity to attend Notre Dame University.

Prior to his GTU enrollment, Kelly had told the archbishop he did not want a parish assignment and that he had sought the degree in psychology to be better qualified to counsel those at the San Mateo Council on "Religion, Grace, and Social Concern." Their object was religious community support for social causes.

However, when Kelly returned to St. Mark's that June, he received a letter from the archbishop appointing him to a parish in Marin County. Kelly called the archbishop to remind him of their agreement not to assign him to a parish when he returned from the GTU.

Displeased, the archbishop punished Kelly by delisting him from the archdiocese official directory. In Kelly's words, he became "missing in action". Kelly returned to St. Mark's Parish in Belmont, where he shared a residence with Pastor Dave Walsh. The pastor was "good to me and let me do what I wanted." At St. Mark's, Kelly was able to pursue his progressive approach to Church ritual and practices.

This out-of-the-way Belmont church was first housed in a converted general purpose warehouse on Old County Road up against the Southern Pacific commuter and freight railroad tracks. Kelly began changing Sunday rituals and customs around dramatically. He told this author, "We did our own thing. We used the basic Mass structure but rewrote much of the liturgy according to weekly themes and brought in secular readings as well as scripture readings. We had a fantastic singing group performing nonstandard music. The place was jammed, but no longer really officially 'Catholic.' The pastor wasn't really into it but for a while he let me do it."

Kelly's former Serra student Red Moroney and Moroney's family followed Kelly from Serra and started attending church at St. Mark's. Moroney recalled, "Some thought Kelly's approach a bit radical but it was a wonderful, forward-looking parish, liberal in both the political and religious respect." At one point, Moroney's family organized a funeral at St. Mark's for a child with Down's syndrome. Kelly presided and, as Moroney recalled, "he talked about how much this two-month-old child had gotten out of life. It was so moving how he brought meaning to this little baby's life…."

Many other folks who had protested the discrimination at St. Matthew's followed Kelly to St. Mark's and supported his changes to the Mass ritual. Sunday Mass became a celebration; afterwards, those in attendance enjoyed coffee and brunch. Some St. Mark's parishioners, however, thought Kelly was breaking too many Church service and worship rules.

Finally, in response to complaints, the exasperated St. Mark's pastor suggested a Saturday afternoon or Sunday evening Mass where Kelly could "implement his own way of performing Masses but still meet the requirements of an official parish Mass." No matter how many parishioners he drew in, Kelly said the "old school" folks at St. Mark's were never pleased.

To celebrate his parents' fiftieth wedding anniversary, Kelly wrote a Mass for them from beginning to end that was "nowhere in the book (of Catholic ritual)." A number of priests who were friends of Kelly's family came to the Mass, and the following Monday morning Kelly received a call from the archdiocese office to schedule an immediate appointment.

A day later, the bishop's secretary arrived at St. Mark's and scolded Kelly, asking him, "What right did you have to change the Mass around? You left this out. You left that out." Kelly asked him, "Did you look around to see if people were enjoying this experience?" The secretary's answer: "That's beside the point!"

Kelly, at this stage, was clearly into doing his own thing and creating a Mass for the masses that was more a celebration of music and joy than tradition would allow. Soon, guitars and drums took the place of sacred organ hymns.

Believing he was acting true to his Catholic spirit, Kelly continued St. Mark's weekend duties and officiated at many weddings and funerals, making lifelong friends along the way. Pam Frisella, former Mayor of nearby Foster City, California, was one of those friends. She told this author:

> On New Year's Day 1977, my husband Danny, a 1963 Serra High School graduate, died in a dune buggy accident. We were living in Arizona at spring training where he was playing for the Milwaukee Brewers; our son was three years old at the time. My husband went out on a dune

buggy and didn't come back. After his death we came back to San Mateo because I had met Danny Frisella there on a blind date in 1970. I decided I wanted to bring him back here for his funeral. I was thirty years old and seven months pregnant. People called me and said that Danny would want Father Kelly to handle the funeral. I met John when he walked into the funeral home wearing his Roman collar, a nice-looking man, maybe fifty years old.

Frisella added:

The homily he gave at my husband's funeral made it sound like Danny was going to go to this fabulous beyond. John said Danny was a person who had lived life and died the way he lived – having fun in a dune buggy. John consoled me during the worst days of my life.

If John hadn't come into my life that day, where would I be or what would I be doing? There is fate and a direction and a path that I am on and if I had not run into John, I don't know what path or direction I would have taken.

Shortly after the funeral, Kelly told Frisella that even though she was Lutheran, she could attend St. Mark's Church in Belmont and take communion. She did so, and through Kelly, Frisella met future NFL star Tom Brady's parents, Galynn and Tom Brady Sr.

Like Frisella, Tom Brady's mother, Galynn Brady, was pregnant. Galynn came to the hospital to visit when Frisella had Daniel three months later on her late husband Danny's thirty-first birthday. Through tears, Frisella remembered:

> John was there with me all the way, bringing me a sense of peace. I just remember it so well – that sense of peace and hope that there was to be more to life. John brought me back from: *I don't know how I am going to do this, to: I'm just going to do it.* And there was never a doubt after that that I was going to be able to move on with my life.

Later on, Kelly baptized Frisella's newborn son, Daniel, and Galynn's newborn, Tommy Brady. Daniel and Tommy later played football together at Serra High School.

Frisella's life continued to intersect with Kelly's. In September 1977, with her new friend Janet Jones, she attended a Cursillo, a three-day spiritual retreat for laypeople that focused on building Christian community. Kelly was the retreat's spiritual director. Frisella recalled:

> That was the life changer for me. John helped me realize it's not about me, it's about how I fit into this world and the connection with people and with my faith. The retreat was probably the single most important way that my life changed. I learned that if you look in the mirror you know

that even if you are loved by no one else you are
loved by God.

She added, "John baptized our kids; he officiated at our mar-
riages; he was there for our funerals; everybody on the Peninsula
has a John Kelly story."

During this time, Kelly hosted a twenty-five-year anniversary party for his tenure as a priest held in the large St. Mark's
banquet hall with many families and friends. By this time, most
people knew, as Frisella put it, "Kelly had had it with the priesthood," and so the anniversary party turned into a community
"roast" of Kelly.

FOUR

Kelly Turns in His Collar

THE YEAR WAS 1979. Pope John Paul II visited Poland, leading to the Solidarity Movement. He later visited the United States. Iran turned fundamentalist Muslim and took American hostages. Mother Teresa of Calcutta was awarded the Nobel Peace Prize for humanitarian work. And Kelly left the priesthood wondering how he might advocate for social justice.

Pam Frisella, Janet Jones, and close friends had formed a St. Mark's Kelly support group that met every other Sunday night with Kelly, who saw his departure coming. Their conversation more and more became about Kelly's unhappiness. They saw Catholic Church bureaucracy stifling Kelly so much that he had lost his glow and his ability to touch people. They knew that ever since he had taken his stand at the St. Matthew's discrimination protest, Kelly would continue to fight for what he believed. The ongoing question became, "What is he going to do?" Finally, one night, after six or eight months of Kelly asking himself, "Should

I, or shouldn't I?" Janet Jones said, "John, do it or forget it." Frisella believed Janet had called it like it was.

Kelly rightly feared leaving the clerical cocoon. He had never really taken care of himself in the world. His family supported him until age thirteen and during summer breaks; then the Holy Mother Church fed and housed him for the following twenty-five years. He had a premonition of his upcoming struggle for survival in the secular world. No wonder he dithered with his life-changing career move. Vatican II changes were going on, and Kelly was encouraged by those reforms; they helped change his whole attitude, but still he hesitated.

His struggle became increasingly apparent to Dolores Homs, St. Mark's Church secretary, as she watched Kelly's transition from priest to non-priest. Homs told this author Kelly was talented and smart and looked deep into his feelings about leaving the priesthood: "He was looking for answers," she said, "and eventually, he found them."

Kelly became more and more involved in local activities outside of officialdom and reached the point where the Church no longer fit who he was. The social concerns group Kelly worked with weekly was almost all lay people. He thought the clergy were getting left behind by lay folks, especially when it came to helping the poor, the imprisoned, the disadvantaged, and the disenfranchised.

Kelly finished his last St. Mark's Mass with a flourish as he removed and dropped his cassock while singing "Born Free." Some insider friends were not surprised, but for most in the congregation, this was their first look at the *real* John Kelly. The generally progressive congregation loved his bold and final act. Others were shocked and dismayed.

Of course, Kelly's bold move had just rendered him homeless and jobless.

After word of Kelly's final irreverent priestly act became known to the archbishop, he offered Kelly a year's leave of absence with pay, perhaps to minimize the scandal. Although Kelly knew he would not return, he accepted the leave, which provided a monthly stipend of about one hundred dollars.

No longer eligible to stay at St. Marks, Serra principal Mike Peterson, ever respectful of Kelly, came to his rescue. Peterson allowed Kelly to live in a small room in one of the school buildings so he would have a place to sleep. He had transitioned from the Church womb only to the birth canal.

Kelly had no idea what he would do for a living. He survived only on his stipend and a bit of money from counseling. His last stipend check arrived in August 1980 with an official exit document. Now, he felt really hopeless. His personal identity went down the drain along with his self-worth. "I didn't know who I was," he told this author, "from a load of hay."

During this time, Kelly dropped by to see his architect brother Michael at Michael's office in San Francisco. Michael told him, "You just walked in like you are the weakest human being, like you are hopeless." For a long time, Kelly felt exactly the way his brother described. He had walked out of an established life into a virtual vacuum.

Certainly, Kelly had not been a conventional priest, but being a priest was all he knew. "All of a sudden I didn't know who I was," he later said. It reminded him of his childhood days when his mother's harsh treatment caused him confusion about his identity.

As a priest, Kelly had never thought much about the deference and even adulation he received—it came merely because of his spiritual status as a priest. Kelly had often warned younger priests not to give up their identity and independence, but he was now forced to concede that priests had to sell their souls to the organization of the Church in order to succeed in their vocation. Kelly had identified completely with the priest role; it had become his existence. He hadn't maintained a broader vision of reality. His priesthood had been the source of all his attention and positive reinforcement.

Soon after Kelly left the priesthood, he lurched into a social vacuum as the number of people who stayed in touch with him dramatically dwindled. He saw how important the imagery of clergy was for many people. Some must have believed they had an inside spiritual or social track with him as a friend. Frisella confirmed the falloff of those Catholics who only wanted to associate with *Father* Kelly. She told this author, "There was a lot of hurt in John that many did not recognize. It didn't mean jack to me that John was a priest. He was just my friend."

Suddenly, people he considered friends who invited him to their dinner table as a Catholic priest and a valued guest didn't do so anymore. His social life disappeared. People didn't call him anymore.

Now with few remaining friends, Kelly recalled that he felt like "a fifty-one-year-old teenager who didn't know what in the world was going on, what I was going to do to survive." He tried receiving counseling to deal with his depression and rage and to vent the ill feelings he had been stuffing away for years. He told this author, "I was angry as hell because of all that I had denied as being part of me."

Parishioner and friend Jerry Forbes said when Kelly left the priesthood, he believed many people were upset with him, and many were. Kelly went through a difficult time trying to figure out who was on his side and who was not. Forbes didn't see him much, not at Mass or church events. But after a time, they met again through a retreat, which Forbes thought was a turning point because it was around this time that Kelly began acting more like his old self.

Frisella said that unfortunately, Kelly didn't leave the Church in what would have been deemed "the proper way." She told this author, "There must have been a blacklist in the San Francisco Archdiocese that read, 'Do not talk to this man because he did not go through the right channels.'"

To be sure, Kelly didn't ask for permission to leave the priesthood; he didn't follow administrative protocol—he just quit. Sometime later, the Serra school hierarchy considered hiring him back to teach. But the day he went to sign the employment papers, the call came down from archdiocese high: "Is that *the* John Kelly, the former priest? No, no you cannot hire him."

To attempt to ease his transition, Kelly tried attending a few churches in the area, including Glide Memorial Church in San Francisco. Once in a while, he popped into other churches on Sunday, but he never found anything that fit. Yet slowly, Kelly began to deal with his anger and depression and started to enjoy life more.

Kelly reflected on his heroes of the past who had overcome difficult times, such as Martin Luther King and Gandhi. He credited their examples with helping him get through his grief and anger and with deciding to move on with his life. Paraphrasing Gandhi, Kelly said, "I will not make anybody my enemy; no matter how different I may be, or how opposed I am to what they are doing, there is something about them I can connect with." Having these larger-than-life mentors reinforced for Kelly what Jesus was all about. One passage paraphrased from the Bible stood out for him: "Don't get caught up with goods and property. Help people and forgive."

Starting Over

Kelly still had a few friends but no job, few marketable skills, and no source of income. He had moved out of his room at Serra and rented a cheap attic apartment in San Mateo. Friend Tom Brady Sr. knew a businessman who ran a San Mateo company, and Kelly was hired as a courier delivering documents for the company in the East Bay.

Starting in 1982, Kelly delivered the documents from 6 a.m. until around eleven in the morning. The job wasn't challenging and had no future, but it paid his bills. Unfortunately, the job also left a psychological scar.

On March 24, 1983, Kelly drove over a hill on I-580 from Hayward to Pleasanton in the East Bay. He told this author, "It was raining like hell and my car hydroplaned, crossed the double divide space, and hit a car coming up the hill." Every March 24 thereafter, Kelly would relive, as he put it, the "unbelievably traumatic experience that killed the driver in the other car." Following the accident, Kelly was hospitalized with damaged vertebrae and shattered nerves, but he hadn't broken any bones. He lost his job and survived on disability and unemployment insurance for a number of months.

For Kelly, the real pain was his responsibility for the death of the other driver. He wondered what the tragedy meant. How had it happened? What had he done wrong to cause it?

Every day and night, Kelly, weeping at times over the accident, would think, "Oh, God, what a horrific experience." He knew the man killed was a fifty-one-year-old father with two children. Kelly agonized over whether to make contact with the man's family, but he ultimately decided not to and never changed his mind. That chapter for Kelly ended with survivor's guilt as well as time to reflect as he recuperated. And now he was out of a job again.

He reflected on one of the few marketable skills he possessed: his knowledge of psychology, gained through his education at the Graduate Theological Union. He had met some men at a Cursillo spiritual retreat, the Catholic unity weekend, who ran a counseling office in Belmont. He contacted them, and they offered him part of their office space to set up a small counseling practice, but he helped only a few people as not many sought his services.

Kelly asked himself where this new path would lead. He thought maybe he could build up the counseling practice, but it didn't feel particularly useful or challenging enough. He wondered, "Should I live my life comfortably as a counsellor or should I become involved in something more meaningful?" Little did he know one of the most meaningful defining moments in his life lay straight ahead.

This happened when friend and community activist Sylvester Hodges asked him, and he agreed, to oversee a free dining hall venture at nearby King Community Center. The job paid little and wasn't particularly challenging, but Kelly enjoyed helping feed poor people, and it provided him a small office as an operating base.

Previously, at St. Mark's Parish, Kelly had had parishioners prepare food boxes for the poor at Thanksgiving time. He had also started a second help group in San Mateo where eighty volunteers filled boxes packed with hearty meals. In a way, he was now continuing these earlier efforts, just in a more organized fashion.

Kelly's new role operating the dining room for Hodges led to the opportunity for which he is best known: involvement with the organization providentially known as Samaritan House.

John Kelly with mother Elly and older brother Ray.

First-grade Kelly and brother Ray.

John Kelly age eight with brothers and dad, Raymond.

Eighth-grade John Kelly (second from left) and brothers.

Kelly in the minor seminary.

**Kelly (in there somewhere) 1954 San Francisco
priesthood ordination ceremony.**

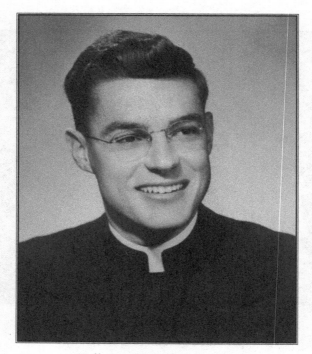

Kelly as new Catholic priest.

Kelly's first vestment photo.

Serra High School—Kelly in classroom.

Serra High School faculty-senior basketball game hook shot.

COMMUNITY SAMARITAN

A good Samaritan is not simply one whose heart is touched
in an immediate act of care and charity,
but one who provides a system of sustained care.
James A. Forbes

FIVE

Samaritan House,
Feeding the Hungry

JOHN KELLY, EVER searching for answers about where he was headed in his post-priest days, recalled that some 2000 years earlier, Jesus had told a story to his Jewish listeners, who typically held their nearby Palestinian Samaria neighbors in low regard. As described in the Gospel of Luke, a lawyer stood up and tested Jesus, saying, "Teacher, how do I get to heaven?" Jesus then asked him, "You know the law. What does it say?"

> The lawyer answered, "'You shall love the Lord your God with all your heart, with all your soul, with all your strength, and with all your mind; and your neighbor as yourself.'"

> Jesus responded, "You have answered correctly. Do this, and you will live."

But the lawyer, desiring to justify himself, asked Jesus, "So, who is my neighbor?"

Jesus answered with a story of a man traveling from Jerusalem to Jericho who was mugged by robbers. They stripped him, beat him, and fled, leaving him half dead. By chance, a Jewish priest came that way, saw the victim, and passed him by. A Levite came to the same place, saw the man and also passed him by. But a Samaritan traveler, as he came to the victim, was moved by compassion and patched up his wounds with oil and wine. He loaded the man on his donkey, brought him to an inn, and took care of him. The next day, before the Samaritan left, he gave money to the inn manager, and told him, "Take care of this poor man. If it costs more, I will reimburse you on my way back."

Jesus asked the lawyer, "Which of these three men was a neighbor to the traveler who was mugged?"

The lawyer said, "The man who showed mercy on the victim."

Then Jesus said to him, "Go and do likewise."

Little did Kelly know that he was about to "go and do likewise." As he would later recall, it was simply meant to be.

Feeding the Hungry

John Kelly later made it sound like he was roped into the leadership of Samaritan House. Rather, it was a marriage of convenience. He had been divorced from his previous role as priest but continued to feel the call to help people in need.

Sylvester Hodges had begun the process by hiring Kelly to run the soup kitchen at the King Community Center in San Mateo's North Central minority neighborhood. That program was called INCH (Interfaith Network for Community Health) Hospitality Family Kitchen, and it opened on April 11, 1984 to serve dinner to thirty-two hungry people. They set up the kitchen and started serving dinner two nights a week with the first King Center food coming from St. Anthony's Dining Room in nearby Menlo Park.

Close by was a little community service referral agency called Samaritan House. It was run by three City of San Mateo workers in a space shared with the Salvation Army. Hodges, who had recently hired Kelly, was heading a search to find someone to implement a proposal to expand and coordinate the efforts of the referral agency. His committee sought a high-energy person with vision and a commitment to moving forward—someone who had community contacts and was willing to work for peanuts. In one meeting, a half-dozen prospects were considered, but none fulfilled the requirements. Finally, Hodges said, "We have been looking at the forest for a tree and we have the best tree right in our own yard." The committee all knew exactly who he had in mind.

They anticipated Kelly would say no, so they put together a convincing plan and voted in favor of it at that same meeting.

At the next one, when Kelly arrived, they explained how hard the committee had worked on the criteria and selection of candidates. Hodges later recalled, "John complimented us and asked about whom we had chosen. As President, I told him how excited and confident we were in our choice and that *he* had been selected unanimously."

As expected, Kelly urged the committee members look for someone else, but they convinced him to take the position on a trial basis. Hodges said later that Kelly's long, successful tenure with Samaritan House proved the committee "picked the right person for the job."

The three original city-paid community workers were joined by a group of volunteers. Hope Whipple Williams, who later ran the San Mateo City Senior Center, initially supervised the three city employees who were joined by a county-paid fourth.

Kelly became director of the county core agency Samaritan House. Williams had known and admired Kelly when, in his previous incarnation as *Father* Kelly, he provided office space and helpers to prepare holiday baskets. They had had so much fun, the volunteers asked if they could deliver baskets to some of the needy families. Williams told this author, "Kelly had a way of attracting and energizing volunteers."

As the new Samaritan House director, Kelly had a primitive little office in the back of the Turnbull Elementary School gym (now College Park Elementary School), part of the San Mateo/ Foster City district. Overcrowding soon prompted Kelly and his cohorts to set up a portable building on vacant school grounds at the corner of North Humboldt Street and Indian Avenue, which became the first official home of Samaritan House.

Sue Lempert, a former San Mateo Mayor and school board member, is a columnist for the *San Mateo Daily Journal* and has long been active with the League of Women Voters. She first met Kelly while she worked for the non-profit Human Investment Project (HIP). Lempert said he came to her Age Center Alliance and to other non-profits offering to help the really underserved through Samaritan House. She had seen firsthand the pockets of hungry poor in the county, and the Alliance was quick to accept.

Kelly soon discovered that hunger was not confined to the area around the King Center dining room. Evelyn Taylor, principal of North Shoreview Elementary School, told him that she knew of families on the east side of town with no meals for their kids. Later, Samaritan House started serving meals at her school twice a week, and within a couple of years, they were serving meals five nights a week. Kelly told this author his friend and partner Evelyn "was amazing and...had so many great things going."

As he began to expand Samaritan House's outreach to different communities, Kelly had plenty of help from others. Peggy Myers from Hillsborough was a great calming influence on his governing board. She and two friends, Eleanor Kauffman and Jane Goldberg, had started the organization known as Breadbasket, which is still in existence today. The purpose of Breadbasket was to help feed children at Turnbull School. They visited different food markets and told the managers they were starting a food program for needy people. Aware that the markets threw out an incredible amount of food, the two women said they would be happy to pick up their leftovers.

Some market contacts were cooperative, but some said they were not interested and that they were worried about insurance and liability even though they were covered by the school's liability insurance.

Safeway and Molly Stone's Market became basic sources of the Samaritan House dining room meals, meaning Kelly didn't have to spend that much money on food. Volunteers who visited the markets delivered everything to Ruby Kaho, the Samaritan House Kitchen Manager who "could really run a kitchen" according to Kelly.

St. Anthony's in Menlo Park had committed to provide meals for Kelly's dining room for six months for free. Every day, Kelly sent a volunteer down to Menlo Park to bring food to San Mateo.

But Kelly knew they couldn't use this model forever. Even though St. Anthony's helped early on, and grocery stores participated with their surplus, it became necessary to raise funds to support the growing population of those in need.

Initial support had come from the City of San Mateo and San Mateo County along with a grant from the Peninsula Community Foundation, but more was needed. Kelly started fundraising around Christmas 1985 with volunteers sending out some three hundred letters. He began giving speeches at service clubs and churches, and gradually, Samaritan House began to build their support base. More and more volunteers came to work at the dining room.

Kelly initially kept track of everyone who showed up for meals, and a box was provided where people could contribute funds. After three months, he abandoned the effort to keep track of the need or eligibility of those who showed up and opened the door to whomever came in. He felt if someone was willing to spend their nights at a community table, he didn't care who they were.

At North Shoreview School, children as well as adults visited because Evelyn Taylor encouraged entire families to come by for a meal. She knew everyone connected to her school and their backgrounds, and she encouraged the families to reap the benefits of Samaritan House.

Due to his reputation and personality, Kelly attracted volunteers from near and far. Walter Heyman, retired CEO of Alumax and a long-term Samaritan House Board member, and his wife and son initially served food on weekends and holidays at a school dining room. Heyman realized Kelly clearly needed administrative help and told him he could do more than just ladle food. Kelly responded that housing and feeding the poor were the two areas where he needed organizational help.

Heyman believed building the food supply would be easy. All he would need to do was write letters to the CEOs of food companies and ask them for damaged food or food that had bypassed its sell-by date. He thought Samaritan House could store it and use it. He wrote the letters but didn't receive any responses. He logically thought one CEO contacting another would warrant an immediate response, but he received nothing.

Undaunted, Heyman, much to Kelly's surprise, then formed a committee of people all connected in some way to the food industry—an owner of a confectioner's shop, a restaurant owner, and the folks from Village Pub in nearby Woodside. The results were immediate, he told this author: "Then we got food by the ton. It was a fun and active committee."

In 1989, Samaritan House added a second mobile building to create a new kitchen. Kelly attracted talent from his Board and knew a restaurateur who set up the kitchen equipment. He recalled, "This fellow and my Board volunteers knew what they were doing. They put together a production kitchen and the committee members helped select and obtain the equipment for free or at a very good price. We wound up feeding something like five hundred persons a day at various locations."

For many years, Kelly, who continued to attract help for his cause from all walks of life, held a successful annual fundraiser in a giant temporary tent in San Mateo Central Park. Nearly every year, Dennis Berkowitz and his wife Janis from Max's Restaurants brought and served the prepared food. For no cost, they provided a crew of over twenty paid workers along with many volunteers.

Kelly later loved to tell the story of board member Bill Schwartz, a local physician, regarding a different sort of food fundraiser. Every year, Samaritan House had a turkey drive asking folks to bring fresh or frozen turkeys for Thanksgiving distribution. They had collected and filled a big outside walk-in refrigerator with turkeys, and one night, somebody broke the lock and stole all the turkeys. The *San Mateo Times* wrote about the heist, and about three times as many turkeys as were taken were given to Samaritan House. The birds were delivered suddenly from those who were aghast at what had happened. Schwartz then suggested "an annual turkey heist."

Additionally, Samaritan House home delivered meals to families and shut-ins. School locations became unavailable, and meals were then served at the San Mateo Westside Church of Christ and at San Mateo Masonic Lodge. Meals were also sent twice a week to serve locations in South San Francisco, the Innvision Shelter Network's Family Place [now LifeMoves], and other locations—kind of a "Meals on Wheels."

As his operation moved forward, Kelly, always expanding his vision, had also realized early on that a key to landing support for the fledging Samaritan House was making the public aware of its mission. Kelly told this author that he believed they were the first (or close to the first) agency to distribute a newsletter, a quarterly that let people know who they were. He said, "We just told the stories and put an envelope in there if people wanted to contribute, but we didn't ask them for money."

To accept donations, Samaritan House had a P.O. box in downtown San Mateo, and the week after they sent a newsletter, the mailbox was jammed. Kelly credited a woman named Lucile Hilliard, telling this author, "She had ten or eleven kids; she was one of our first volunteers at our dining room. She used her expertise as a newspaper person to put the newsletter together. She was fabulous." Then those at the Board of Realtors printed the newsletters for them free of charge.

Kelly was amazed at the community support he was receiving. He knew that he had found a new vocation that was meant to be, one where he could help people—those who were lost, those who were poor, those who were hungry. The many blessings he had received, like Hilliard creating the newsletter text and the Board of Realtors printing it for free, were no accident. Much was due to Kelly and the myriad of community volunteers whom he was able to attract. "Those kinds of things kept happening," he told friends. It was amazing. Samaritan House was really making a difference in people's lives.

The City of San Mateo powers-that-be initially showed great support with general fund contributions but switched funding to special funds. Kelly told Jim Nantell, then Assistant City Manager, that he saw "the handwriting on the wall." Kelly knew that when government budgets were cut, Samaritan House funding would be reduced or cut.

Sure enough, by the early 1990s during a financial crunch, some City of San Mateo council members questioned why they were spending so much money on Samaritan House. At that point, Kelly had been forced to, as he told this author, "every bloody year go around and talk to every city councilperson to maintain our income." He dreaded doing so and decided he had to take action.

Through Kelly's efforts, and eventually the efforts of an active board of directors, Samaritan House fundraising became so successful that they no longer needed government money as a primary source. "That made all the difference in the world," Kelly told this author. "My philosophy on human service was if you are going to be effective, be based in the community; get the community to support what you are doing, and make the community...not only the energy but the fiscal supply as well."

To that end, Kelly and his board created many programs conducive to volunteerism, so eventually they had "six, seven, eight hundred people a month" doing something for Samaritan House. When there was a government financial crunch, Kelly would boast, "You may suffer, but we don't have to suffer because we are paying our own way."

Kelly's political philosophy was, as he joked, "to have government involved as little as possible—in anything. So that made me a Republican!" Kelly believed that the problem was that "the private sector had less interest in really doing its job. So, we fell back on Democrats who were at least pretending they were setting up services. Unfortunately, they developed bureaucracies that didn't work and consumed resources and so we were stuck with nothing."

"The unique thing about Samaritan House, and to some degree Shelter Network and HIP Housing, was that we were a private non-profit run by the community," Kelly told this author. Every single board member was involved in developing some part of their program. Dr. Bill Schwartz, for example, championed the idea for a health clinic. They had Louis Weil, Dennis and Janis Berkowitz, Walter Heyman, and many other community people committed to the organization.

What made the board members and volunteers special, Kelly believed, was that "they felt a sense of ownership; they were part of what Samaritan House was doing. The amount of attention we got from people once they were connected with Samaritan House was amazing."

Kelly, his baritone voice booming as it once did in the pulpit, would talk to groups and convince them to invest since community investment was what made Samaritan House unique as an agency. Kelly also networked and contributed by serving on the Shelter Network board of directors and interacting with the Second Harvest Food Bank in Santa Clara.

Pam Frisella recalled, "John sort of brought all of us into the fold. He became 'Mr. Samaritan House,' and it blossomed. He wouldn't take credit, but he built it from its embryonic stage through many stages thereafter."

Frisella added, "We had the passion because we saw people not eating; we were out in the community. I didn't write big checks, but I was out there." By this, Frisella meant she was involved hands-on in the homeless shelter, while others would personally tackle additional areas of concern within the community.

When Samaritan House ran low on funds, board member Walter Heyman said Kelly picked up the phone and called "an ex-student or somebody he married or whose child he had christened. That was his way of raising funds." In addition to its many community and agency contributors, Samaritan House had, through Kelly's efforts, over two thousand volunteers who often also developed into donors. In any case, they certainly had an alliance with the agency that was a lasting one. Even if they just handed out toys at Christmas, a real relationship developed. That was significant because, as Kelly later recalled, "when it came to fund raising—ten dollars or a hundred dollars—they all participated."

Bill Kenney, a San Mateo attorney and another early Samaritan House Board member, served for eighteen years. Kenney met Evelyn Taylor while serving on the San Mateo/Foster City Elementary School District board during the 1970s. Later, Evelyn was President of the Board of Samaritan House and asked Bill to join. Kenney and Kelly both had Serra connections. Kenney had attended high school there before Kelly's arrival.

Kenney is Catholic and was on the National Cabinet of the Guidepost Foundation for the Norman Vincent Peale Church. He believed in tithing and the gospels but, like Kelly, realized what was what important was "how we make this spirituality work in the modern world. How we help people." Attorney Kenney expertly counseled Kelly on legal issues, always joking that his advice was "worth exactly what Samaritan House paid for it—nothing."

The attorney told this author Samaritan House team did "God's work in feeding the hungry and taking care of the poor, and we had to trust in God that the money would come. I believe that God sees to it that the money does come." Kenney's prescient advice to Kelly was "don't depend on government money. So, we didn't. We basically relied on the community for money." Samaritan House submitted grants for public funding for community counselors and for the permanent homeless shelter, but Kenney and Kelly's philosophy of financial independence never wavered.

"The board held an annual retreat, but the resulting strategic plan really didn't make much difference because John did what he wanted and what he and we thought would work," Kenney told this author.

Kelly and the board worried a great deal about their temporary kitchen and office facilities and what the landlord school district might do if they were to need the school land and terminate the lease. Possible loss of their headquarters and entire operation was a perennial concern.

Bob Fitzgerald, a longtime and active board member and former Foster City Mayor, admired Kelly's optimism and confidence "that if we did good work, financial support would be there." Fitzgerald recalled that in the early 1990s, they held a number of board meetings discussing two key issues: lack of predictable funding and Kelly's insistence on more and expanded programs to meet the ever-growing needs of the community.

Fitzgerald told this author, "His optimism was catching! We expanded a number of programs, especially the hot food distribution and medical clinic. We even started looking for a building to buy, so we could expand our services."

Kelly told people that he could never have accomplished what he did at Samaritan House if he had still been connected with the Catholic Church. "By the time you received permission to blow your nose, you couldn't do anything," he told this author. When they wanted to expand the clinic next to St. Anthony's Church in Menlo Park, he recalled, "The pastor was all gung-ho, the church council was all gung-ho," but Kelly had to ask permission from the San Francisco Archdiocese. He made contact and in return received a letter asking what their position was on abortion and birth control. Kelly told them, "I am not going to get into this; forget it. I am not going to waste my time."

Kelly's friend Brian Cahill ran Catholic Charities in San Francisco. Kelly told this author, "Brian went through more than his own share of hell because he was trying to allow certain people [members of the LGBT community] to adopt children, and he had issues around [support for] birth control." Cahill in turn said, "Kelly had a classic line: 'If the Church gave up its hang-up on sex and dealt with injustice, they might actually accomplish something.'"

By leaving the Church and his vocation behind, John Kelly had helped build Samaritan House and by doing so helped thousands of needy people. He had organized programs that fed the hungry and along the way helped many individuals one by one. His talent for assisting the many was exceeded by his loving concern and attention to troubled souls and to individuals who needed his personal care.

Six

Albert Odom Success Story

JOHN KELLY'S LIFE is punctuated with stories about those he helped. As he began his work in the temporary San Mateo City Samaritan House, he chanced upon a trouble-prone young Black child.

Albert Odom was in second grade when he met Kelly at that original Delaware Street location. Kelly later set up the first Samaritan House office and kitchen on the far corner of San Mateo Turnbull School land where he had frequent encounters with Odom.

In a cramped, makeshift kitchen, Kelly and his volunteer crew prepared grocery store discards into meals for the hungry at the school hall after school let out. In the economically struggling neighborhood, a group of mostly Black kids used the playground after school to practice basketball.

On Tuesdays and Thursdays, these kids came by later for free dinners, then all hustled out to play ball. Later, Kelly recalled,

"These boys were trouble; they gave me a bad time. Albert Odom had four brothers, same mother but five different fathers. The boys lived with their grandmother until she died and they returned to live with their inattentive mother." Odom told this author that they slept in cheap motels with welfare vouchers where his mother's boyfriend kicked the seven-year-old out of bed, and he was forced to sleep on the floor.

Summarized through Albert Odom's eyes, he told this author how Kelly rescued him from what would surely have been a life packed with turmoil, likely a life of crime:

> I'd known John since I was in second grade. When Samaritan House was on Delaware Street, they had this kumquat tree. In my backyard the fences all connected and we'd walk down the fence and steal the kumquats. John told us to stay off the fence. Samaritan House also had an entry ramp and we'd ride our skateboards up and down that ramp.

> I'd been in a lot of trouble in first, second and third grade at Laurel School. I got kicked out of Laurel and John and his good friend Principal Evelyn Taylor transferred me to North Shoreview School where they could watch over me. If I messed up in school, I knew Mrs. Taylor and John were always there.

> Samaritan House at Turnbull School gave my grandmother bags of food and I ate dinner

there with my mom and grandmother. At ten and eleven o'clock at night, some friends and I broke in and stole ice cream and sandwiches from the unlocked refrigerator. Still in the third and fourth grades, that showed what kind of parents we had to still be out.

Once when ten or twelve of us were playing after dinner, John pulled just me into his back office. I felt like I was in big trouble, maybe even with the police. John told me, "Look, don't break in here. You guys can have the leftover food—just help clean up. Earn what you get. Do me a favor and I'll do you a favor." So, I helped clean up, mopped the floors and put the tables up and was able to take the ice cream and the extra food home.

I started doing very good in the fourth grade when my grandmother died and my life went topsy-turvy. I became a real problem and not just for my mom. She tried to take care of me and my brothers but she was on drugs and drugs run your life.

I lived for two years in Los Angeles with my dad who had come home from prison. He went back to prison and I came back to live with my mom who had welfare vouchers to stay at the Royal

Lodge Motel. I started selling drugs in middle school and still got into a lot of trouble.

I spent almost a year at Hillcrest Juvenile Hall, went to trial and ended up in CYA (California Youth Authority—jail for juveniles) when I was fifteen. After about four months I got a letter from John saying he had been trying to find me. I didn't have anybody but John, who started coming to visit and write to me. It felt good. I felt wanted. John always made me feel wanted. I always felt appreciated. He was never just some passerby who'd help you and then move on.

After three years, I was supposed to get out but nobody in my family would let me stay with them. I was calling everybody and they were saying they didn't want that trouble. And I was a troublesome kid. I could have again lived with my dad in Los Angeles, but my dad was a gang banger and the stuff I was doing here would have been made worse in Los Angeles.

My cousin LaRonn and John helped me get out of jail in January of 1996. Back in San Mateo John found me a job—my very first job ever, at Wisnom's (now Ace) Hardware. John told co-owner Dick Nelson about the whole situation and Nelson took a chance on me. I picked up skills and a trade and learned how to build barbeques. Dick helped me get my first driver's license. In a year and a half, I learned a lot. It was great. I've only had two jobs in my life and Wisnom's was the first. I was there for a year and a half when things went downhill.

In 1997, still on CYA parole, I got picked up for associating with a friend from CYA who was arrested for drugs. I was sent back to CYA because technically I had come in contact with police. Back in CYA I was angry because I hadn't done anything. I was held at (CYA) NRCC in Sacramento through my birthday, through Christmas and through my wife's birthday. At the end of three months, John came to my Parole Board meeting with me.

At the Parole Board meeting I was told to leave the room. I don't know what happened between Parole Board officer Leon Panetta and John but I think he asked John, "Would you trust him inside your house?" John told him yes and Panetta said, "I believe you can be released because this gentleman (John) says he would trust you inside his house. And I trust him." I'd gone in December 2, 1997 and I got out February 18, 1998 and I've never been back since. I remember running back to get my stuff and all of us walking out to the parking lot. I

was so thankful for the conversation that went
on between Panetta and John.

Odom returned to his North Central San Mateo neighborhood and his old job, leaving criminal activity behind. Chief of
San Mateo Police Susan Manheimer told this author, "Odom,
whom John mentored through a childhood of likely violence,
certainly felony behavior, terrorized and influenced other youth
in a negative way and spent time in and out of prison. This young
man came back out a changed individual. He spoke at Rotary
and was a compelling and inspirational speaker. John introduced
him to the Leadership San Mateo Program, really giving him the
chance that he'd never had."

Manheimer added, "All laudable, right? In Leadership
Program, young Odom started getting a bit more critical of issues
(especially racial profiling). We had some concerns that he was
still involved in some of those earlier activities. I talked to John
and said it was not appropriate to bring him back into the civic
culture without him committing to no longer misbehave and to
no longer negatively influence the young kids out there. They
were all looking at him as a role model. So John and I had a big
disagreement about that. He thought I was being a hard-assed
cop, which I was. I thought he was being the weak liberal, which
he was. I respected his position and I understood.... It was almost
like a prosecution and defense."

Odom maintained that he had matured a lot and said that
he had started a family:

> When we started neither my wife nor I had credit
> so John let us use his credit for our first car, my

first motorcycle, and for our first apartment. He's really been a part of my life and then also my wife's and kids'. Kelly called me one of his adopted kids and a great father to my two sons.

I told John that if he had stayed a priest, he could have been a saint. John saw good in people and said, "If you want good to come out, stick with me." I lived to impress him, to do good. He came over to my house and played with my kids at birthday parties and other guests commented that John was the only white guy there. "Who is that, the school principal?" John just sat there and cracked up and played with the kids.

When we went out to lunch we'd look around and laugh at the people watching us wondering what we had in common. I don't know exactly what it was with John, just that he is a very selfless person. His whole goal in life was [to make] the world...a better place.

Saving Odom's life was entirely in keeping with John Kelly being the quintessential good Samaritan: here was a man who, as James A. Forbes once said, was "not simply one whose heart is touched in an immediate act of care and charity, but one who provides a system of sustained care."

SEVEN

Clothing the Naked; Housing the Homeless; Healing the Sick

P OOR PEOPLE LIKE Albert Odom and his family needed food and love, and Samaritan House met those needs by providing dinners at food kitchens and delivering food baskets to their homes. They also needed clothes, so Kelly, a superb organizer, suggested Samaritan House form a clothing donation for parents and children.

Twice yearly, Samaritan House held "Super Saturday" giveaways. Initially, the giveaways were held in a school gym, then in an unused warehouse, followed by the Purple Palace, an old house painted purple that they shared with sister non-profit Shelter Network. As need kept growing, they moved to a rented building across from North Shoreview School. Eighty-year-old Lucille Francard stepped in and became the volunteer boss of the Clothes Closet.

Department stores would have envied Francard's management of her five female workers. During the 1989 Bay Area earthquake, roof timbers at the Clothes Closet fell, narrowly missing Lucille, but she soldiered on, cleaned up the disaster, and returned to business. Soon they needed an even bigger space to meet burgeoning demand. This effort turned into a major Kelly challenge.

In 1994, Kelly and the board located a building on South Claremont Street, San Mateo. They applied, and the city approved a zoning/use change from retail to warehouse, but the city planning commission required a community meeting to alert the neighbors about the change of use.

Kelly knew that private citizens everywhere wanted the homeless to be clothed for cold winter nights and, not incidentally, to look presentable when encountered on downtown sidewalks. But he also knew many citizens believed anything remotely associated with homelessness should happen elsewhere and "not in my backyard."

The ex-priest thus braced himself since he knew the homeless clothing plan would meet resistance despite the property being a block from train tracks and adjacent to industrial and auto shop uses. He told this author he prayed, "Lord, make sure you keep me safe," before he attended the meeting scheduled at nearby Sunnybrae School. "Two to three hundred people showed up, mostly young families."

Attempting to remain calm, Kelly tentatively entered the packed school hall and immediately encountered an elderly man standing by the door. The man gave a quasi-polite hello to Kelly but then scowled and said, "If the original owner of this building knew what you were doing, he would turn over in his grave." Kelly didn't comment; he just moved forward into the school gym to address the crowd.

The meeting went downhill from there. Kelly recalled that almost as soon as he began his presentation, people began screaming at him "for ruining and destroying the neighborhood." One woman shouted to the group, "Well, I've already seen two homeless people sitting in their car just waiting for the Clothes Closet to open, and others like them are going to be coming like crazy."

Kelly took the criticism in stride, never raising his voice. Although the meeting ended without resolution, he knew that in order to keep the neighbors happy, a myriad of city rules and regulations would be required about how the place was run. For instance, no one could travel unaccompanied by staff from the winter homeless shelter to the Clothes Closet building; another rule stated that on Friday, singles day, a community worker would drive the homeless person there, wait until they obtained their clothes, and then drive them back again.

After some time passed, Kelly, the peacemaker, felt relieved and vindicated as he told this author, "Following the initial objections, we never ever had an official complaint from a neighbor about how we ran that building."

During this time, a true defining moment happened regarding the Clothes Closet. A local wealthy lady in her late nineties had no relatives except a niece who never paid her any attention. She told her lawyer, "Find me some charities that I can give my money to." The lawyer's wife suggested Samaritan House, and when the woman died, she left the organization enough money to buy the building. The Clothes Closet building has since been closed and sold with the proceeds used for a new larger building. Samaritan House now operates the replacement Kids' Closet in their renovated main building on 42nd Avenue and Pacific Boulevard in San Mateo.

Housing the Homeless

Initially, Samaritan House provided temporary housing assistance using the California Army National Guard Armory, across the street from Samaritan House's makeshift headquarters. The armory became a shelter at night, and in the morning, Samaritan House cleared all the bunks out of the main hall so the army could use it during the day. The armory shelter residents did not have to be clean of drugs, but they had to be willing to participate in drug and alcohol cessation programs. They could stay for as long as six weeks.

The shelter created a very contentious situation for residents of the San Mateo North Central neighborhood where the armory was located. The residents complained about people hanging out, being dirty and responsible for crime, although Kelly claimed, "Many of their concerns were unfounded."

San Mateo City Council member Sue Lempert said that the city funded Samaritan House at thirty- or thirty-five thousand dollars per year and assigned some shelter duties to city staff to assist the homeless effort. While that was a blessing, Kelly recalled that funding shrank during lean revenue years and grew later and that these variations made it difficult to budget and support the shelter.

Another San Mateo City Councilman, Jerry Hill, believed the operation of the homeless shelter presented too many problems for the neighborhood and wanted it closed or moved. The armory capacity was limited to ninety individuals per night, but sometimes a 120 lined up outside. The doors opened at 5 p.m., and those who didn't make the cut were turned away to wander the neighborhood all night, "presenting problems for the residents."

The next morning at 7 a.m., the ninety individuals had to leave the shelter. But they didn't want to go far because they had to be in line early to be included in the ninety for the next night. Many roamed the neighborhood, camped out at the nearby Martin Luther King Community Center, or hid away out of sight.

Hill voiced his concerns to Kelly on numerous occasions. Kelly, in turn, invited Hill into his world to see how poor people struggled to survive and how various challenges brought them to homelessness. Kelly explained that many homeless suffered from substance abuse, unemployment, or mental or physical illness and had little support or help to turn their lives around. The armory was the best available site that at least offered shelter from the nighttime winter weather.

Kelly compassionately focused on one poor soul at a time, and Hill understood meeting the need. Still, he was concerned about the ill effect on the surrounding neighborhood. Hill told this author, "I gained an understanding of the homeless problem, but I also wanted to resolve some of the neighborhood issues. The area around the armory was teeming with homeless people and the neighbors wanted some relief." Deciding to become involved, Hill worked with Kelly, San Mateo County Supervisor Ted Lempert, and county staff to develop stricter operational controls for the use of the armory as a winter shelter. They used a non-profit charity gathering place, St. Vincent de Paul, to distribute ninety shelter vouchers each day, which eliminated the lines to enter the armory. Hill also encouraged bus operator SamTrans to provide daily bus passes, so the homeless could leave the neighborhood area for work or other reasons and not congregate. These operational moves resolved many neighborhood concerns.

Later, as an elected San Mateo County Supervisor, Hill recalled, "Working with John, South San Francisco Mayor (the late) Gene Mullin, and SamTrans, we located a homeless shelter site at the SamTrans bus maintenance facility near the airport." Much to Kelly's relief, Hill also helped cobble together necessary project funding to create the facility. Kelly told his author, "The result was that we had a ninety-bed, year-round homeless shelter in San Mateo County which was largely self-sustaining." [Author's Note: it is still in existence today.]

HEALING THE SICK

Samaritan House community case workers became aware of clients, particularly the undocumented, non-U.S. citizens, who were not receiving sufficient medical attention.

In 1989, board members Drs. Bill Schwartz and Walter Gaines were both practicing at Mills Hospital, San Mateo. In private practice since 1961, Schwartz had always felt disappointed that he could not take more care of indigent and needy patients. After reading an article by Kelly in the San Mateo County Medical Bulletin reporting that Samaritan House really needed a clinic, Schwartz contacted him. The two discovered their mutual interest in aiding the needy and decided to see if they could to build a clinic from the ground up. With help from Drs. Schwartz and Gaines, Kelly formed a committee to explore starting a Samaritan House free health clinic. Dr. Gaines and especially Dr. Schwartz became the spark plugs for the medical clinic.

Board member Bill Kenney told this author that birthing a medical clinic was a quite a challenge for Samaritan House, but he believed creating it was what the organization was supposed to be doing: "[I told Kelly,] 'Let's take a chance on it and see what it is like,' and so that's what we did. And John was always willing to go along because he too felt the Divine Providence the way I do. The medical clinic was a big step forward. It was a stretch and risk for the organization."

According to Schwartz, Kelly was a goal-oriented person with "tremendous leadership skills and a good partner in the clinic project. He told me, 'This is where we want to go. I can't get it done alone. You and whoever you work with are going to have to get us there.' And we got there because Kelly wanted us to get there. Much went without words. At the Samaritan House board meetings, Kelly was there and on my side."

Schwartz first thought they would receive assistance from the San Mateo County Hospital. "But they were worse than not helpful because they would say, 'Yes, that is a good idea and we will do that.' But when it came to the reality, they weren't there. It was, 'Oh no, we can't do that.'"

For example, Dr. Schwartz wanted to coordinate medical records with the hospital and asked for a copy of their blank charts. Their answer was, "Oh no, we have to get permission from our hospital board of directors."

Dr. Schwartz practiced at UCSF Hospitals as well as at Mills-Peninsula and therefore thought it strange that it took "two or three years before they would license me at the county medical center." He believed from the beginning that the clinic was a wonderful idea, but the big lesson he learned and passed on to Kelly was that the county hospital was not really interested in competition, especially competition they didn't understand.

Dr. Schwartz also believed the county hospital administration feared a free clinic might take care of needy people who might otherwise be paying patients at that hospital. The loss of patient revenue could threaten their jobs.

The county hospital demanded to be paid for their services, and Kelly and his committee nearly said, "Let's just forget it." Schwartz had to agree: "Some doctors on the county hospital board of directors really didn't approve of a free clinic and blocked it, but they didn't want us to think that was happening."

Cordial relations with the hospital finally settled in, but Schwartz, backed by Kelly and the Samaritan House Board, told this author that in the meantime, he "moved the county hospital folks aside and talked to others to obtain support and find a place for the clinic." What was initially a $25,000 liability insurance issue was resolved when Mills-Peninsula Hospital covered them under their umbrella insurance policy.

In 1992, the clinic was finally created using a room in one of Samaritan House's temporary portables on Humboldt Street. During the day, the room was used for meals and all sorts of uses. In the evening, like changing the set of a stage play, tables were pushed aside, and other tables were brought in along with partitions and curtains. Initially, this humble venture was in operation only one evening a week, eventually increasing to a few more nights a week, and after five years, they decided the clinic needed its own space.

They rented an office space on North San Mateo Drive. Sheryl Young, later CEO of Community Gatepath [now abilitypath], had connections with Mills-Peninsula Hospital and helped obtain the space at very low rent. Dr. Walter Gaines took on the task of getting the new clinic declared official, funding the clinic's own insurance policy, and expanding the number of doctors who could work there. Kelly later recalled, "That paperwork amounted to the founding of a brand new hospital." The clinic, one of the first of its kind in the country, flourished.

Bob Merwin, CEO of Mills-Peninsula Hospitals, provided the new free clinic essential laboratory and x-ray services. Dr. Schwartz recalled, "Bob was extremely helpful all along the way. When the hospital received new equipment and furniture, Merwin gave the surplus to the clinic, resulting in a very amicable relationship with Mills-Peninsula Hospitals." The hospital also recruited Mills doctors and nurses to work at the new clinic for free.

Schwartz told this author, "We were actually able to reduce costs because we took care of many patients early in the course of their illness so they didn't become sicker and end up in the emergency room with its $10,000 bill." They also treated people with communicable diseases which might have spread into the community if the clinic was not there.

At a clinic promotional presentation to the League of Women Voters, an upset audience member asked, "Are you encouraging all these people to come across the Mexican border to your clinic?" Like Kelly, an advocate for social justice anytime or anywhere, Schwartz defended serving undocumented immigrants and said, "They are part of our community and the clinic doesn't ask whether or not they are legal. They send their children to school and if they or their children are ill, as doctors we have a responsibility to take care of them. We don't ask questions because we are a local community and we are not setting policy for the state or the nation."

Soon thereafter, the clinic started recruiting specialists so they could deal with all kinds of illnesses as well as general medicine. Kelly recalled CEO Merwin boasting that Samaritan House clients were receiving the best care on the peninsula. Eyecare was added and Rotarian Gerry Bundy of Bundy Opticians provided glasses at no cost. The clinic also started providing dentistry, and according to Kelly, "That was really unique in the world."

Predictably, the rental space again became too small and crowded, and Samaritan House then purchased and moved into a free-standing clinic building at 19 W 39th Avenue in San Mateo. "Buying and funding that building in 2000/2001 was very important," Kelly told this author. "We raised the money to pay for the building. In fact, Peninsula Health Care District gave us a fair amount of money to help pay for it."

The clinic medical staff volunteers were committed and generous, sharing many hours of their time. Dr. Schwartz recruited physicians who were retiring and said the doctors felt "rejuvenated because they could do real medicine. They had no paperwork to worry about, and they could spend as much time as they wanted with a client. I had more doctors tell me that the greatest thing that ever happened to them was to volunteer at Samaritan House."

A great spirit was generated in the clinic, and Kelly told this author that "the psychological healing that went on there was as important as the physical healing. Can you imagine the good feelings of these people who had no other possibility of real medical care?"

Dr. Schwartz cherished the thought that when Kelly felt overloaded with his many responsibilities, he often drove to the San Mateo clinic to watch the caring and dedicated staff do their job. He told this author, "John would just look around, but he felt great joy about what was going on. He soaked up the good will."

Kelly called it "getting refurbished—rehabbed. If you walked into that building on 39th Avenue, you'd just feel it walking in the door; the spirit there is fabulous. And Bill Schwartz had a lot to do with getting it all set up and generating that spirit." Curing the sick one vulnerable human at a time made Kelly proud of their newest clinic and lifted his spirits.

In late 1999, an editor at *The New York Times* somehow heard about the Samaritan House health innovation and sent a reporter to check out the free clinic. The reporter stayed for two days, and on December 5, 1999, the Sunday edition carried a front- and second-page article with pictures about Samaritan House and the health clinic. Subsequent articles were published in *Modern Maturity* and *Parade Magazine*, and the clinics were also featured on ABC's *Evening News* with Peter Jennings, PBS's *California Connected*, and CNN's *Democracy in America*.

Dr. Schwartz said one lesson he stressed to Kelly was to "leave government out of it. Do as much as possible with the private sector." However, the Director of Sequoia Health Care District, a tax-supported quasi-government agency, contacted Kelly and wanted to create a similar clinic in their area. Kelly and his board thought an exception to the "leave government out" rule was warranted and agreed to help.

After a short search, they found a suitable building at 114 5th Avenue, Redwood City, and, as Kelly told this author, "Sequoia pretty much covered the whole expense." Dr. Schwartz said that the Redwood City process was much easier than the San Mateo project "because we had the Sequoia Health Care District behind us one hundred percent. They were lovely people to work with and we had excellent help and got it started in relatively short order." Samaritan House Free Clinics were then, and still today, providing medical and dental help to low-income and uninsured individuals in much of San Mateo County.

Kelly beamed when anyone mentioned the Samaritan House free health clinics. Yes, he knew his belief in it made a difference, but it was the steadfast work done by the doctors, especially Bill Schwartz, that made it happen, another indication of how members of a community may band together and make a powerful impact on the lives of thousands of people.

JOHN KELLY MOVES ON

By the end of 1998, Kelly, along with many supporters, had transformed the fledgling effort called Samaritan House from an embryo into a major independent non-profit. It operated the ninety-bed homeless shelter, two free medical clinics, and a free kids' clothes closet, as well as fed 145,000 meals a year to the hungry. An amazing 2,000 volunteers helped provide these services to some 15,000 needy people in San Mateo County, California.

As noted, most of the funding continued to come from private donations, which insulated the operation from the vagaries of government funding. Ever the innovator, Kelly was ahead of the curve regarding government budget cutbacks and set the stage for a fiscally solvent and sustainable organization. "Local citizen funding and volunteering helped the community take ownership of the operation," Kelly told this author. "Samaritan House's startling growth and success served as 'a model of neighbor helping neighbor.'"

Now aged sixty-nine and after nearly fifteen years at the helm of Samaritan House, Kelly found himself once again exhausted during the 1998 Christmas crunch time. The years of hard work had tired him out, and dealing with the holiday season rush was no longer something he looked forward to.

After some thought and prayer, Kelly decided his goals and wildest expectations had been fulfilled, and it was time for him to move on and for someone else to take over. Samaritan House had grown in complexity and now required many of the administrative duties that Kelly had chafed against in the Catholic Church.

In early 1999, with some sadness, mixed with pride in what he had accomplished, he submitted his resignation.

Kitty Lopez, a former elementary and high school teacher, child psychiatric consultant, and current executive director First 5, became Kelly's eventual successor as Samaritan House executive director. She thought that at some point the organization's bureaucracy had become too much for Kelly. Lopez was the perfect person to take over. She had learned from long association with Kelly and continued to carry out his crusade to assist the poor and underserved.

"John was very good at bringing people together," she told this author, "including the volunteers and getting the community involved. In my mind, Samaritan House always had two missions: one is to help people in need and the other to create a community that helps people in need, and we all do that together. That's what John believed and what I believed."

Board member Walter Heyman agreed that Kelly was never an administrative whiz. He was always in charge and achieved important things, but his desk and office were chaotic. Heyman said that you could not see the top of John's desk, which was "covered with a good eighteen inches or more of letters and manuals and paperwork." Not only was Kelly disorganized; Heyman recalled that Kelly hated administration and that it showed. "When he retired, it took him three weeks to clean off his desk. He knew where everything was, but no one else did."

Regardless, Kelly was justly proud that he had run the organization with an almost skeleton staff to keep overhead low. He was primarily concerned with providing maximum benefit to the poor, even if administration suffered.

Kitty Lopez said when Kelly's Samaritan House ran the homeless shelter, they took people that most organizations would not accept since Kelly believed they should take anyone who showed up. But Lopez, when she took over, looked at it through the lens of the whole organization to ensure everybody was safe, including at the shelter. She told this author, "John didn't worry much about that; he cared, but he was so busy making sure we helped everyone that organizational safety wasn't a priority at times."

Lopez recalled that accommodating ninety homeless people (many of whom had just been released from jail or were on probation), accommodating the shelter staff, and keeping everybody safe was an ongoing issue. But she added that when she and the staff worked with Kelly, "he ultimately acknowledged that we had to keep safe."

As county probation and welfare agencies continued to try to figure out how to integrate those just released from jail back into society, Kelly maintained the idea that people can change for the better and that their lives can be different. He believed released prisoners should be given the benefit of the doubt and a chance for a new start.

When Lopez became executive director, she knew there were some "employees who were trouble or unqualified and who had to leave," but Kelly "always gave everybody a break. It didn't matter if they had credentials or were qualified or had the skills. Kelly asked me, 'Can you get them (or keep them in) a job?' I asked, 'Can they do A, B, and C?' Kelly responded, 'No, but they need a job—give them a chance.' I often had to say, 'John, this employee is on drugs and a danger to others; we can't have this person or this type of person working for the agency,' and he accepted my advice."

Lopez and Kelly had similar views about people and about the community, and according to her, Kelly's message was always that "we were here to help each other. If you had extra stuff and your neighbor needed it, you gave it to him. If you needed a place to stay and I had a couch—come on over. That's how he operated and how he acted on that simple message about helping people, especially in their time of need. And Kelly built that in the community."

The board decided after Kelly retired that they had to remove him from the spotlight to give Lopez a chance to become the new face of Samaritan House. To that end, the board gently moved Kelly away from any significant role.

Kelly struggled a bit with the transition to new management and the more business-driven approach. Volunteer-driven for most of its life, Kelly had run Samaritan House with four people, and it drove him crazy that there were now six executive staff and perhaps a score of other paid employees (and still many volunteers). Board member Pam Frisella said that she realized that the organization had grown much bigger and complicated over the years, requiring professional staff. Regarding Lopez as the new executive director, Frisella said, "She did an absolute fantastic job taking over the good work of John."

Looking back, Kelly claimed and few believed that organizing and running Samaritan House was a project he had become involved in not strictly by choice. "My arm was twisted to run the dining room; the county twisted my arm to take over the Samaritan referral service." But Kelly did take some credit, saying, "I was able to somehow pick out knowledgeable and dedicated people to work with at Samaritan House." Kelly recalled that he and the board of directors battled at times, but even so, he stated, "God, were we blessed. We had some of the most fantastic people on our board."

Kelly certainly deserved credit for his willingness to work hard to spread the Samaritan House message. He spent countless hours, morning to night, broadcasting what they were doing and gathering valuable support in the community. He never had a spare day in his life while at Samaritan House. He confessed to friends that there was "some value in my not having a family of my own. I could never have spent all that time building and running Samaritan House if I had had a wife and kids at home."

Kelly was justly proud of his contribution to Samaritan House's unrelenting efforts to feed, shelter, and care for the health of the county's poorest residents. No matter how large the organization grew, Kelly somehow treated each person served as if they were his only concern.

EIGHT

Education and Service to Youth

JOHN KELLY ALWAYS had a special place in his heart for youth. He counseled and guided them, first as a Serra High School teacher then as the leader of Samaritan House. Walter Heyman told this author that Kelly was big on education and often partnered with North Shoreview Elementary School Principal Evelyn Taylor to improve opportunities for young people.

Samaritan House, encouraged by Kelly and Taylor, always offered educational youth activities; they paid attention to elementary school children and made sure they were on track to attend college. Heyman said, "They had the kids spend many hours outside of school for additional education opportunities and made sure that the parents were involved with their kids."

Kelly worked a great deal with PAL (San Mateo Police Activities League)—typically volunteer and assigned police officers serving youth in trouble with the law. Kelly's help included tutoring them and coaching them in soccer. He knew to do things differently with disadvantaged young people so they didn't wind up in gangs and in prison.

After Kelly left his leadership role at Samaritan House, he continued to be involved with education, particularly to counsel and inspire underserved and minority kids. One example was Kelly's work at Bayside Middle School, which was 90 percent low-income Hispanic.

Dick Nelson, former co-owner of a successful San Mateo business (and employer of Albert Odom), worked alongside Kelly at Bayside and its STEM (Science, Technology, Engineering, and Mathematics) Academy in east San Mateo. This school had been adopted by the San Mateo Rotary Club of which both Kelly and Nelson (and this author) were members. Both Kelly and Nelson personally tutored and mentored Bayside students. Nelson said that the students of Bayside respected Kelly because "they knew he meant it when he made them say in unison, 'I am going to college.' He was very serious about how they studied."

Kelly made use of his earlier Latin and English teaching experience by helping Bayside students write their assigned papers. Kelly had a calm but firm way of telling a student who was playing around to get back to work. He recruited student tutors and kept them returning and setting good examples for their student charges. He reminded both tutors and students to do a good job because a Rotary scholarship could be in their future. Kelly was known as more than just a teacher; he had a direct and engaging style that earned students' respect as a mentor and human being who clearly cared about them.

Kelly bugged school administrators about the lack of available counseling in a school where many kids had "a horrible life going on at home." The faculty was trying to teach them science, technology, engineering, and mathematics, but many students were unable to eat breakfast, lunch, and dinner.

"It was all wacky," Kelly had told administrators and anyone who would listen, "that our elementary schools didn't have major counseling departments. For every kid who walks into one of our east-side-of-town schools, we should know exactly what their family situation is. What are their challenges? Why are they having all these problems? There are stories in the *San Mateo Daily Journal* about some of these kids who are going to college and some of what they had to go through to survive." Kelly asked, "But other than these few, who in our school system or in our community is paying attention to these kids?"

Those Bayside students appreciated the fact that Kelly sat down with them one-on-one and took the time to find out about their family life and how they were going to survive when they began high school. Jeanne Elliott, Principal of Bayside Middle School and STEM Academy, asked Kelly to meet with two youngsters in particular once a week for counseling. Kelly told this author, "One kid didn't come back to Bayside—I wasn't sure he'd make it. I expected to see him some day in San Quentin; the kid hardly had a chance. He had a horrible life. Some of these so-called parents—they were biological and that's it. They were on drugs and booze. At least, one of the kids did well in high school and went on to community college."

To show his love for his students, Kelly once interviewed every eighth grader at Bayside Middle School who was on the San Mateo Academic Rotary Team (SMART). Older students who succeeded in the program tutored younger students. This ongoing program encouraged promising eighth graders who did not (and whose families did not) expect to attend college to instead take college prep courses in high school and then enroll in a two-year or four-year college. Like Kelly, many Rotarians regularly met [and still meet] with their SMART students individually during all eight high school semesters to encourage and help keep them on track.

Kelly visited the school twice a week to encourage these middle school students. Principal Elliot recalled that "he especially decried the loss of proper grammar and the limited writing skills of the new generation. He defended Latin and all language proper...yet he was cool."

Kelly recollected that he had begun conducting Rotary scholarship interviews twenty-five years earlier, and back then "it was all boys and a sprinkling of girls who applied. And a girl would never say she was interested in math or science." Later he read a current feature in the *San Mateo Daily Journal* about high school kids, including girls, going into engineering and math—it was a whole different world. When he conducted his last Rotary student scholarship interviews at Abbott Middle School, there were twenty-seven eighth-graders who applied—twenty-five girls and two boys. One of Kelly's favorite lines was, "The male of the species is slowly getting run over and they don't know it is happening!"

Kelly, ever watching the times as they changed, wondered how much school districts' decisions were driven by socioeconomic considerations. He told this author about "how the people on the west side of town controlled the city schools and that's where all the resources went." And he questioned, "Who was doing all the talking when you went to a school Board of Trustees meeting? Was it anybody from the poor east side of town? Who represented them? There seemed to be no energy toward making things change."

When Kelly was director of Samaritan House, along with his close friend Principal Evelyn Taylor, the organization provided eastside North Shoreview School $10,000 a year for "extras." That amount was insignificant compared to what west side schools had "where the PTA or PTSA did all that extra fund raising. If we didn't help, the North Shoreview kids wouldn't have had anything."

Kelly believed that some schools on the west side should have adopted some poor schools on the east side since "there were a lot of things that needed to be changed" on the east side.

In addition to being involved at Bayside and Abbott Middle Schools through the Rotary, Kelly became a board member and an advocate for youth through the Police Activities League sponsored by the City of San Mateo and run by then-Chief of Police Susan Manheimer. Manheimer had been familiar with Kelly's involvement at many different schools and his focus on challenged youth, including those incarcerated at San Mateo County Hillcrest Juvenile Facility. She had a vision of turning the Police Activities League from a prevention program for all kids to a program specifically focused on youth who already had been first time offenders and were in gangs, so she invited Kelly to join the board. He accepted.

Once on the board, Manheimer never expected that Kelly would become for PAL "such a critical role model, mentor, advocate and trusted ally for our troubled youth." She said he would be there "when all of other board members and staff had wrung our hands and said we could no longer deal with a youth. Even when kids had gotten into serious trouble, Kelly mentored and tutored them and said, 'That's OK, we won't forget about you.' He stayed in touch with their families."

Manheimer further told this author, "What Kelly did was so not for recognition. He helped troubled individuals because it was the right and important thing to do." He intuitively and instinctively knew what the "needs of needy people were; that included me at times. When I'd been so downhearted about a youngster that we'd worked so hard with—he'd notice and minister to my needs, while also being mindful of that young person."

Kelly was a parent to everyone. Manheimer continued, "That's something you can't fake. It truly comes from the spirit and heart." Kids automatically turned to him when they were in need. "His unconditional love was more than a policeman's love; sometimes it was more than a coach's love."

Manheimer cautioned that sometimes what was needed was tough love and believed Kelly was incapable of tough love. She added, however, "there always had to be the one unconditional loving grandparent around. And that was John for our entire community." No matter how successful and accomplished you were or how dire in need you were in a prison, in a youth group, in Juvenile Hall or just dropping out of the programs, that "grandparent" John would help you. "I saw him just work miracles."

Nevertheless, because of their different approaches, Manheimer sometimes was crosswise with Kelly. She told this author, "I had to put limits on." She said she was the parent who exhibited "tough love" and made sure a kid was out of the gang and that there were consequences for kids' actions. Kelly was not there for the consequences; he was there just to be their advocate, which she conceded is one part of the PAL youth development model.

The "consequence" part of the Police Activities League was to "approach as if a youth wants to play rugby or soccer or tap dance or volleyball—that's great, but here's your social contract. You need to get out of the gangs. You need to get back to school. You need to improve your grades."

For kids with multiple generations of bad-influence family members, it took a long time to steer them to the right track. Kelly, however, helped them progress by leaps and bounds solely through his love and understanding, almost like, as Manheimer described it, an "inoculation and there was only one John Kelly vaccine." She knew that he built kids' self-confidence by saying, "Whatever it is that you've done, there is a reason and purpose and a highest calling for you. Let's find it and let's get there."

Through its volunteers and staff, PAL advocated, "Get out of the gang and become the PAL gang. PAL will invest in you, provide you with playing fields, get you in a soccer league, and provide you with uniforms."

Coach Leroy Miranda had initially been hired to help develop a PAL soccer team at San Mateo High School. The targeted team prospects were young gang members in San Mateo High School neighborhoods looking for a way out of the Norteños and Sureños gangs. At one PAL board meeting, Coach Miranda was asked how he would implement his soccer plan, and he said needed someone to work with the kids and who could speak their street language. Kelly spoke up and said, "I'll do it." Manheimer recalled that she looked at "this sixty-five, maybe seventy-year-old white guy, wanting to hang out and coach the San Mateo Sureños [Gang]." She thought he was "a well-meaning

PAL Board member, but at the time, I didn't yet know the magic of Kelly."

The board did approve Kelly's involvement, and he would walk over from his nearby Samaritan House portable offices to the practice area and watch the start-up soccer activity for a few weeks. Kelly reintroduced himself to Miranda, saying he knew nothing about soccer but that he wanted to watch. While Miranda taught soccer, physical conditioning, and teamwork, Kelly later said, "I looked for an angle to help the kids find their inner selves and to motivate them to learn and improve."

After watching for a while, Kelly approached the team and asked the soccer kids how many had a Social Security card. They laughed since more than half had not been born in the United States. After he knew the kids better, Kelly offered a spare Samaritan House room next to the practice fields as a way to fulfil the academic improvement part of their PAL contract. He provided simple books for the kids to read but discovered they could barely make it through a sentence and the others made fun of the mistakes. Miranda told Kelly, "The kids didn't want to read, and they couldn't write in English or Spanish."

Kelly could only hold their attention for fifteen minutes until Miranda brought snacks, saying, "If you feed them, they will come." Sure enough, they came and stayed.

Coach Miranda told this author, "John was very straightforward; he'd be very honest with you, and the kids took to him. John began to know some of the boys better, and they started to put more effort into their work. After about six months, the players would walk over and, as a sign of respect, greet Kelly, 'Abuelo, (Grandfather), what's doin'?' They would tease John about his poor hearing and about John's common expression,

'Oh stop it,' eventually buying him a t-shirt with that expression written on the back."

Kelly started following up at their school across the street. He knew the San Mateo High School Principal (and Rotarian), Yvonne Shiu, and she approved his showing up periodically during the day to check on the kids. He would walk around, talk to Shiu, and ask how the team kids were doing. He made trips to the library and taught the kids where the Youth Center was so they could find out about college. Many of these kids had never been in the library, much less a career center.

Kelly pushed all the time, asking, "How are your grades? Show me," and "Is your homework done?" If they hemmed and hawed, he would say, "No excuses, I want to see it." When a kid received a good grade, Kelly made it a point to let everybody in the group know, and everybody would clap. That's when Miranda and Kelly knew things were starting to change and that they were really making a difference.

One day, a lost and floundering Korean kid named Dook showed up at soccer practice. He knew a couple of the boys who had been in the program for two years, and they had encouraged him to come out to the field and just have fun. He was reluctant and said he didn't know how to play soccer. But Coach Miranda talked him into giving it a try, gave him his own soccer shoes, and began teaching him the basics.

Dook couldn't look Miranda or Kelly in the eye and hesitated when Kelly asked how he was doing in school. Kelly asked him to bring him his report card and, as he surmised, all was not well; his grades were poor. Kelly took him to the career center, introduced him to a tutor, and checked on him periodically.

By senior year, Dook could read and speak English and Spanish in addition to his native Korean. He turned all his grades around, and at his graduation in 2010, he gave a very moving speech. He thanked the PAL Program, he thanked Miranda, and he especially thanked Kelly for motivating him and making him feel special, like he could do whatever he wanted. He said that he was lost and didn't know what he wanted to do but "now I know that I am somebody." He brought the audience to tears, and they stood up and gave him a standing ovation. Dook attended College of San Mateo and became interested in a mentoring program.

Not all the minority youngsters succeeded. Miranda recalled, "At one time I had twenty-six boys, but two went to jail, one got shot, and three just walked away from the program." If they wanted to come back, though, he and Kelly welcomed them back. At the end of that first year, they had eighteen boys on the team and on the right track. According to Principal Shiu, two of the boys who rarely showed up for class before entering the program "regularly showed up for class and had raised their grade point averages from under 1.0 to 2.5" after joining the program.

One convincing sign of positive progress occurred when police officers driving down the street would receive a wave from these boys; prior to entering the program, the boys would turn their backs on the police. Some of them did still land in trouble, but they trusted Kelly and Miranda, who explained to them that the police couldn't always be in their corner because if a law was broken, they had a job to do.

During this time, Kelly made several trips to juvenile hall to see one incarcerated youth who had been in a fight and stabbed another youth with a screwdriver. Kelly told him that even though the student was currently separated from the program, the student was not forgotten, and his peers and Kelly were going to stick by him. Both coach Miranda and Kelly took the mothers to the Hillcrest court session and translated between lawyers, court, and parents as the boys' mentors just to show support.

Kelly often counseled the soccer team members by telling them stories from San Quentin about young men, especially those from south of the border, who had made one mistake and were sentenced to ten years to life. They were deemed "hard cases" and were never given a chance at redemption; most courts washed their hands of them and either sent them back to Mexico or to prison.

Kelly told the author, "We needed to fight for the at-risk kids in court to gain that second chance. These were not bad kids. Some were defending themselves in fights. Their prior records showed that these guys were gang members, but the courts didn't see how they were trying to change—how they were trying to turn their lives around. We needed to give that side of the story to the court."

To provide the at-risk boys with real life lessons, Kelly asked San Quentin Prison inmates he knew personally who had taken various self-improvement courses, gotten degrees, and generally turned their lives around to write letters to the PAL kids. These inmates shared with the PAL soccer team members their thoughts about what it was like for them to be in a gang. The prisoners said they initially thought gang membership was the best life—like being in a family. When things went well and there was no trouble, the gang took care of them. But then the moment they were arrested and thrown in prison, all of a sudden, the gang disowned them.

One inmate named Ke, convicted at age nineteen and sentenced to twenty-five years to life, admitted in his letter to the PAL kids that he had committed a vicious gang murder. He wrote that he was "Hella scared" and ran to his gang member friend's house to hide out. His friend said he couldn't stay there. He was arrested, and when he went to trial, his "boys [gang] testified on [against] me." Such letters made an impact; Kelly made sure of that.

A number of the letters explained that though the Norteños and Sureños gangs' might seem like families, gang members were on their own in prison—it was a dog-eat-dog world with no advantage to belonging to a gang. One letter read, "What you think you are going to get with being a gang member, you don't get. There's no love there."

Another letter read, "If you are not banging for the group or selling drugs or killing somebody when you are told to, you are useless to them. This isn't a life for anybody."

The PAL youth took turns reading these letters out loud to their group. Kelly remembered, "It was powerful to watch these young men glean a reality check from the letters."

One young man's eyes watered as he read the letter of a San Quentin man sent to prison for murder on the day his son was born. This young PAL boy had been born out of wedlock and didn't ever have a father figure. Kelly later found out the youngster had grown and had a child of his own and was a great father. He called Miranda on Father's Day to say, "Hi Coach. How's John?" And he called Kelly to ask about Miranda.

Some of these young men's parents were "honest job" gardeners, and the kids helped their fathers on weekends. The mothers frequently did housework and maid service. Miranda called their work "respectable" and he admired it, but he asked the kids if that's what they aspired to be—a gardener for the rest of their lives. He didn't think their parents had that goal in mind for them. Miranda, like Kelly, told the kids, "Show your parents that you will take it to the next level. Get your education."

Kelly promised many of the kids that if they walked across the graduation stage, he would walk with them. He would sing if they wanted him to. He told them, "I'll do whatever it takes to help you graduate." His encouragement often worked—PAL honored two of these students after they had improved their grades from under 2.0 to, in one case, straight A's, and some of the others closely matched that achievement.

Kelly told this author, "Those kids totally reversed what they were before. They could now hold a conversation. Now they would look you in the eye, smile, and converse with you. They'd ask how you were. They even knew how to treat a girl." Respect toward girls was a dramatic turnaround from when Kelly first met them.

When the PAL boys began playing soccer, Kelly was especially irked when they would say "Hey, hey, hey" and whistle when girls walked by the group. Kelly chided them, "What are you doing? They are not dogs." He told this author that he advised the boys, "You want to talk to the young lady, go talk to her. Show her respect. Do you really think a girl is going to come over when you are whistling at her? You want a date? Treat them the way you'd want your sister or mother to be treated." Over time, some team members started enjoying dates, Kelly recalled. "They learned that respect was the key."

Likewise, athletic success for PAL boys came in baby steps. In their first practice game against San Bruno, a local city team, the team was "shellacked" six to nothing. Kelly talked to some of the PAL boys later and they were angry. He told them that they now knew what it took to win. "You lost today. Get over it."

The following week, playing a South San Francisco team, the young soccer players tied two to two then won their next three practice games. They learned that the hard work and confidence building that Miranda and Kelly were preaching actually worked for them on the soccer field and in the classroom. Kelly and Miranda knew it was time to let them play in a league.

The PAL team, in brand-new uniforms, played a home-field rematch with the San Bruno team that had earlier beaten them so badly and won. Unfortunately, the fans were few since many parents worked two or three low-paying jobs to support their families and were unable to attend. Kelly and Miranda, however, filled in as family, fans, and support system, all in one.

Afterwards, the PAL team's opponents, the previously reigning champions, ran over and they all hugged. It was quite a sight to see ex-gangbanger PAL youth sit with young men they didn't know and talk after the game. They were clearly ready to succeed in the local youth soccer league. Sure enough, year one in the league, the PAL team took second place, and year two, they tied for first place.

One August afternoon, a PAL team member's mother came to soccer practice and thanked Kelly and Miranda, saying, "My son comes home now every day after school. I used to worry because before PAL soccer he wouldn't come home until ten or eleven o'clock at night. I knew he was out there with a gang. Now he comes home after soccer practice every day and the first thing he does is ask, 'Mom, what can I help with?' Or if he saw dishes, he'd go wash dishes. He'd help his little brother and sister with their homework."

The mother added, "I want to thank you two. He talks about you all the time." In gratitude, she brought Kelly and Miranda fresh tamales and presented them right there on the field along with a nice hug. The two men agreed that this is what it was all about; even a single acknowledgment from a grateful parent was reward enough for everything they had tackled that year.

Success on the soccer field and at home, as noted, also started showing up at school. The boys had outgrown the little Samaritan House study area and were now getting extra help in regular high school classrooms. With principal approval, the janitor unlocked the rooms after school hours, and over time, the PAL students advanced beyond remedial to regular school work.

The youngsters could now write full sentences on the board and read the Kelly-provided prison letters and news articles about education. From their initial simple vocabulary words to full sentences, they had advanced to writing complete paragraphs. Kelly recalled, "a great dark cloud was leaving them. You could see it in the way they walked and the way they presented themselves."

Most importantly, the PAL team members no longer looked fearfully over their shoulders as they had when they first came to play. They ignored their former gangs and even their former rival gangs. Surprisingly, the gangs also left them alone. Kelly told the boys that as Dean of Students at Serra High School, he had met a lot of great young men, "but you know what, there are no greater young men than the ones I see right here in this PAL group. No one has had to work harder and show greater self-control and effort than you guys have. I'm proud of you—better yet, you should be proud of each other."

Four of the PAL boys graduated from San Mateo High that June. One said that since there were limited tickets, his father couldn't be there, and so he wanted Kelly and Miranda to be there in place of his dad. Both attended, and according to Kelly, "It was like our own sons were walking across the stage."

A week later Coach Miranda and Kelly took the graduates to dinner and the first words out of Kelly's mouth were, "Anybody sign up for college?" Three of them had registered and one was undecided. Kelly warned he would keep pestering the undecided one until he signed up.

A couple of the PAL players were a few credits too short to graduate, so Kelly encouraged them to sign up for adult school to earn their GED. Kelly went to one of the boy's houses and walked him right to school to make sure he was registered for adult school classes. Even after the student registered, Kelly continued to follow up with the student with father-like dedication.

Even some young men who had graduated out of the program and who were now at college came back just to see Kelly. Miranda had called Kelly "Batman" and said he was still his sidekick "Robin." He told this author, "Kelly was a born leader motivated to help people. If there was someone out there who could use his help or inspiration, John would be there for him." John even helped individuals grow socially.

The PAL organization held an annual fundraising awards dinner, and each year Kelly reserved an entire table so he could bring several PAL soccer youths and introduce them to a social environment they had never experienced. They were able to meet wealthy people who donated money and, more importantly, who cared about the success of the program and wanted to personally meet the participating boys.

One year, Kelly recalled, as his young guests were listening to the music and moving to the beat, "Some ladies asked them if they'd like to dance and, sure enough, they danced right in the middle of the place; three of the boys and three women who showed them how to dance. They all got such a kick out of that." Kelly had counseled, "See, these people want to meet you. Open up and talk to people. They will help and people do care. It is not just about the money they contribute."

PAL Board members certainly were willing to help with finances, but they also provided major moral support. When the PAL soccer team won their first championship, it was before the largest audience ever to watch them play. The PAL Board and friends of board members outnumbered team family members and friends.

At a barbecue afterward, the boys felt like celebrities talking about the game and school with people they had never met before. True to form, Kelly walked by and told the boys, "Tell them about the B you got on that paper the other day." And to a supporter, he said, "Talk to this one who hasn't signed up for college yet." The boys didn't mind his prodding because they knew he really cared.

Police Chief Manheimer, as the backbone of PAL, truly believed in the youth program and especially in Kelly's contribution. One year, Kelly realized that the students always lacked school supplies and offered to buy them supplies. But the chief quickly provided funds from her city budget, and Miranda and Kelly went shopping.

These two caring people bought pencils, paper, calculators, and other school supplies, put everything into new backpacks, and distributed them to those who signed up for them. Later, the boys would walk up to Kelly with pride and say, "See John, I've got my backpack with me." Kelly would answer, "Yeah, but is your homework in there? Show me."

Miranda observed, "John knew how to push the right buttons and yet knew how to back off, when to listen, and most of all when to be the driving force. He was first gear; he took you out of neutral, put you in first, and showed you the direction and made sure you shifted into second and third gear. That was John."

Kelly believed there were all kinds of opportunities and chances to counteract what influenced young people into criminal behavior. He especially believed in forgiveness and unconditional love. "Say what you want about immigration and minorities, but if you spend time dealing with these kids, you end up loving them. You realize how good they are and what potential they have."

Ever active, eighty-four-year-old John Kelly was brought to a sudden halt on Christmas Eve 2011. Late in the afternoon, he complained to his friend, Samaritan House kitchen manager Ruby Kaho, that he felt "funny." After talking with him briefly, she became alarmed and called Kelly's nephew Patrick and friend Pam Frisella, who quickly called an ambulance.

Kelly was transported to Kaiser Permanente Redwood City, where, once stabilized, it was determined he had had a serious stroke incapacitating the left side of his body, rendering him unable to walk. Fortunately, the stroke did not appear to affect his brain or impair his ability to talk. After a three-day hospitalization, he was transferred to Brookside Nursing Home near 25th Avenue in San Mateo to begin physical therapy rehabilitation and try to regain his ability to walk.

The PAL members were worried when they learned of Kelly's stroke, and a vanload of fourteen boys went to the hospital to visit him. Kelly could hardly move, but he wanted so much to sit up and show them he was still their strong leader.

As they gathered around his bed, the perennially hungry teen boys couldn't help but notice that Kelly had maybe twenty boxes of candy by the side of his bed—gifts from visitors. He noticed the not so subtle looks and asked them if they wanted a piece of candy, and like piranhas, the boys dug into the candy.

When the youngsters found out that Kelly would no longer be able to navigate stairs and would need to be moved out of his second story apartment, they jumped at the chance to help. Eleven PAL soccer boys showed up as part of a volunteer moving crew to pack up and move his things from his unit to a new handicap-accessible senior apartment in Lesley Towers in downtown San Mateo.

Pam Frisella and Kelly's nephew, Patrick, organized the boys, and they all helped lug furniture and heaps of disorganized books and papers into vehicles. This author came upon Kelly's old, thoroughly worn-out bedding, his lumpy, bachelor-on-the-floor mattress, and much single-man debris and recruited some PAL youth to lug it down the long stairway to a twenty-cubic yard dumpster on the street. A few serviceable things were moved to Atria, his interim assisted-living quarters in nearby Burlingame, and some furniture moved to storage pending Kelly's move to Leslie Towers.

Kelly recuperated over several months and maintained his ability to think and speak. Walking remained painful and recovery was slow, and it appeared that he would always need a walker. However, as soon as he could, Kelly had someone drive him back to the practice field where Miranda reported that the "Pied Piper Kelly had the boys congregate around him and his walker asking how he was." Kelly responded by asking them how they were doing in the classroom.

The boy's mentor and friend noticed there were many new faces on the field and asked them about the new arrivals. They responded, "Yeah, that's my little brother; that's my cousin." The PAL team players believed so much in the program that they were now bringing their younger siblings.

Kelly told this author that he informed them, "I'm going to keep coming out here, and don't think just because I'm on a walker that I'm not going to be checking up." The group moved from the San Mateo High practice field to the King Center to make it more convenient for Kelly and the boys. Miranda noted that John was not about to let what happened to him deter him from helping these kids find themselves. Chief Manheimer agreed and appreciated all Kelly had accomplished.

Manheimer told this author, "I am honored to have known John Kelly, and I am extremely grateful that he chose to take the kids who were really our toughest nuts to crack and recognize we had to do something early. Otherwise they would have ended up in San Quentin and then would have been ex-cons who could fail to ever escape out of that cycle of violence. We invest in our youth, but you know what, we can do all the programs in the world. But until, like John Kelly, you touch a kid's heart and soul and show them unconditional love, you don't really get there."

John Kelly as Samaritan House Executive Director/Administrator.

Kelly as M.C. at the annual tent-in-the-Central Park fundraiser.

Kelly at one of many community events.

Kelly at PAL fundraiser with Scott Pons and Pam Frisella.

Kelly in the Samaritan House kitchen with head cook Ruby Kaho.

Kelly helping PAL soccer players with "catch-up" academics.

NYT article about Samaritan House free health clinic.

Kelly at a quiet moment in an otherwise hectic schedule.

JUSTICE REFORMER

While people in our prisons made mistakes—
sometimes big mistakes—they are also Americans.
We have to ensure as they do their time
and pay back their debt to society
we are increasing the possibility they
can turn their lives around.
President Barrack Obama

NINE

Restorative Justice

JOHN KELLY'S PASSION for restorative justice and rehabilitation versus retribution had incubated and grown during his final five years as a parish priest at St. Mark's Church in Belmont. As he entered the final phase of his life, he steadily transitioned into a full-time social justice advocate.

Toward the end of his tenure at the church, Kelly had often encountered parishioners who had attended Cursillo retreats—weekend-long retreats that taught Christian laypeople how to become effective Christian leaders in an increasingly secular world. Members of Kelly's congregation had often invited him to join, but Kelly would respond that he was too busy, and besides, "it's for lay people and as a priest I don't need it." Cursillo organizers regularly recruited priests to be directors for the program, but most priests reacted like Kelly, insisting that they didn't require additional spiritual development.

Finally, however, Kelly had relented, and to his surprise, he enjoyed his first retreat. He especially liked the intensity and social interaction. From 1976 until he left the priesthood three years later, he was a member of a Cursillo team, including the one noted where in 1977, he led the "life-changer" first retreat for friend Pam Frisella. However, after leading a number of retreats as a priest, Kelly told this author he had counseled the Cursillo organizers, "You don't need us priests—just go ahead on your own. You lay people have more sense than we do." Even so, he had been sold on the weekend activities and continued to be involved in a manner that he could have never expected.

In 1991, the middle of Kelly's leadership time at Samaritan House, Cursillo lay-leader John Carberry asked friends Vic Perrella and Kelly if they wanted to "make a Kairos." Kelly wanted to know what that was, having never heard of it before. Carberry explained that it was similar to a Cursillo weekend but inside a prison. He called it "a weekend of spirituality, literally God's 'Special Time.'"

Kelly told the author his first reaction was, "I'm busy with Samaritan House, trying to get a clinic started, and why the hell would I want to go into a prison anyway? That is the last place on the face of the earth I'd want to be." Kelly and Perrella both thought the request was insane. But later, even though they had some misgivings, they decided to give it a try, and Carberry scheduled them for a prison visit.

On a Saturday, the week preceding their first Kairos, Kelly and Perrella headed north across the Golden Gate Bridge to their orientation at the 400-acre high-security compound known as San Quentin State Prison. Kelly recalled to this author that he felt apprehensive as they approached the security outpost just outside the massive walled building. He relaxed just a bit when he noticed that the San Quentin façade reminded him a bit of the seminary building where he had studied and resided before being ordained.

Kelly expected that there would be thorough security but never imagined that he would be treated much like an entering inmate, being searched for weapons and other contraband. He signed the register and showed his California drivers' license, and a burly guard cross-checked his identification against a pre-approved list.

Once he, Perrella, and a few fellow outsiders were deemed safe and acceptable, iron bars slid open to their left, and he and the others were herded into a sally port. The gate was controlled by a stone-faced guard behind inch-thick bulletproof glass. He closed the entry gate bars to cage the group in an elevator-sized space.

The guard carefully looked them over one by one. Satisfied with his inspection, he opened the bars at the far end of the sally port, releasing them into a short, dimly lit tunnel that opened further into a large open courtyard. This security treatment would be repeated with each of the many entries and exits that Kelly would experience over the coming years.

The following week, with his newly assigned team, Kelly returned to San Quentin to experience his first Kairos. The retreat kicked off Friday evening and continued through Monday night. The program included a series of talks and meditations that volunteers, the "outside guys," gave in a preplanned, structured format.

On day one, the volunteers divided the group into tables of six inmates, the "inside guys," where they were joined by four of the Kairos "outside guys." Each group sat at their same table for all three days. At the end of each general talk, the table groups then spent fifteen to twenty minutes discussing what the message was for each inmate member of that group. Kelly told this author that "Day One was a 'Who am I' type of talk. Then there was a 'Know Yourself' session dealing with that person's view of themselves as a human being and what part they were leaving out and not paying attention to and how did they end up in prison." Kelly said that later on Friday nights, there were "only meditations, which were centered on reflection as to what was said earlier."

"The Prodigal Son" session on day two, Kelly said, "dealt with each of the inside guys being assured that no matter how bad each one felt about themselves, that they could change for the better." Thus, the second day was focused more on forgiveness.

One of Kelly's favorite sessions on Saturday morning was "Choices." It related to each of the inside guys dealing with blame and the understanding that no matter how many people they wanted to blame for being incarcerated, choices were made, resulting in prison terms. But now new choices were possible; there was "the power to change."

Day three focused on ways of changing and how to do so, either in San Quentin or after release. During that Sunday afternoon, each of the outside guys wrote a personal letter to the guys on the inside.

In the evening, when inmate participants returned from dinner, those letters were passed around. The inside guys had no idea that this was coming, so they were surprised and touched. For more than a few of them, it was the only letter they had received during the entire time they were in prison. Kelly recalled that "some of the inmates just broke down; there were Kleenex boxes on the table for the inmates to use."

Kelly told this author that as he sat beside the inside guys, looked into their troubled eyes, and heard their stories, he better understood why they had ended up in what they called the "Q." Kelly certainly had empathy for the victims, a great deal of empathy, but he also realized that if someone, anyone, had just cared about many of these men—family, friends, anyone—there would not have been a crime—no victim and no one to incarcerate. But there had been a crime, and these men paid the price: loss of freedom for years, maybe for life.

One of the inmates said to Kelly, "I bawled my eyes out when I realized the pain and the suffering I caused; I just let go more than I had ever let go in my life." This realization was not unusual among the inmates, especially when they received the letters from Kairos team members and from those who had previously made the Kairos retreat. They were reading letters addressed to them personally, and Kelly said, "All of a sudden they were overwhelmed by the fact that someone cared about them."

Following the letters ritual was a birthday party of sorts—a celebration. The "outside ladies" had baked a huge cake with every inmate's name on it and everyone sang "Happy Birthday" to celebrate what was described as the first day of the rest of each inmate's life. For some, it was the only time they ever had a birthday cake baked for them.

On Sunday evening, all of the inside and outside guys wrote on a piece of paper a list of all the people that they needed to forgive in life. The outside team volunteers produced an empty pot and two lit candles, and each participant approached the ceremonial pot with their handwritten papers. One by one, they held out their forgiveness lists, lit them with the candles, and symbolically dropped them into the pot to burn away. This permitted each person to take a new look at his life after having forgiven those who he believed had harmed him.

During the Monday session, Kelly reported that the inside guys were asked, "Okay, what are you going to do about all this? How are you going to change your life?" And at the end of that day, the inmates were asked four questions: What were you like spiritually when you began Kairos? What has happened to you? What did you learn on the weekend? What are you going to do from here?

Kelly told this author there existed a support movement associated with International Kairos called "You Are Not Alone." People who belong pray for the working team every hour of every day while a retreat is in progress. Before it began, a preassigned support group had written support messages and supplied posters for the Kelly team, which the team hung up on the prison room walls. Team members who were musically inclined played accompanying folk music for the inmates in between sessions.

The Kairos team typically stayed overnight outside at the nearby Protestant Seminary in San Anselmo or at a local Motel 6. Outside ladies had meals and spiritual support ready for the team after they had left the prison and were finished for the day.

Kelly recalled an initial feeling that he was genuinely doing something good for someone who was really down and out. He discovered that the Kairos prisoner insiders appreciated that the outsiders kept coming back and didn't give up on them. Signing up on a volunteer Kairos team included agreeing to come back once a month for a year. An inmate told regular Kairos volunteer Jerry Forbes, "You outsiders keep coming back, so you really must care." Forbes said a lot of other groups visit, give them a "one shot deal, then never return."

Kelly told this author, "The Kairos weekend generated a sense of togetherness and family. By Monday night, you wouldn't believe what had transpired." He described a song called "The Community Song" that included all sorts of hand and arm gestures. Kelly said, "When they first started out singing it on Saturday, the inmates were saying, 'What is this crazy deal?' but by Monday night the inmates were jumping out in the aisle and bouncing around while they sang."

On Monday evening, the inside guys believed the weekend was over and that the outside guys were about ready to go home. Both inmates and volunteer outsiders went to say a final prayer in the Catholic chapel, but then, as they walked over to the Protestant chapel, the San Quentin "guys in blue"—inmates who had made the Kairos before—formed a human corridor for them to walk through, holding candles and screaming and hollering, congratulating their fellow inmates.

When the Kairos inside guys arrived at the Protestant chapel, fifty to a hundred outside people were waiting for the final celebration. The men received a standing ovation as they entered. Kelly later described it as "the most powerful experience I ever had."

Representative prisoners appeared on stage to answer three questions about the retreat. The table families had previously developed responses to the questions and picked a representative to report their collective answers. They each had a chance to share what the Kairos experience was like for them.

Team member Forbes told this author that "of the forty-two inmates typically at a Kairos weekend most had not ever spoken publicly. Most were minorities; many were young men who you knew had never talked to a group. Yet they got up and talked about their Kairos experience. It was enough to make you cry and to make you ask, 'What the hell happened here?' It was so spiritually uplifting."

As the men, many of them very young, spoke, nearly a hundred inside men who had already done Kairos were yelling encouragement and jumping up and down. Kelly told this author, "Oh my God, it was my very first Kairos on that Monday night, and I was crying my eyes out. And that got me hooked."

After that weekend, Kelly and Perrella couldn't resist being at San Quentin as often as possible. Before long, they would travel to the prison two or three times a week. Kelly told this author, "I soon felt very much at home."

Kelly later explained, "The original history of Kairos was to deal with lifers and set up a system where they could learn how to help each other inside after the 'outside guys' left. These were people who were going to be incarcerated for a long, long time. At San Quentin, the program gradually expanded to include not only lifers but also what were known as 'short termers.'"

Recalling his experience, Kelly pointed out a huge gap between lifers and short termers. "With the lifers, a lot of them came into their prison setting and stayed the same person they were before they got there—still playing games, contrabanding drugs, etc. But usually after five or ten years, something dawned on them. They didn't feel good, didn't feel alive, didn't feel human. Something needed to be different. Gradually, they started to want to take a deeper look at what it meant to be a human being. And once that happened, they were ripe for change—ripe for Kairos."

Kelly further explained, "During the first few San Quentin Kairos programs, the volunteer team struggled to get the inmates to take any of it seriously. They'd walk in on a Friday night wondering, 'What the hell am I doing here?'"

After a while though, the Kairos team watched as a dramatic change took place over the four days. It became easier to interest new inmates to join once word spread from those who had participated earlier. Kelly said, "Soon the prison had a waiting list; it became the thing to do. Other than the outside volunteers, the major influence became a nucleus of the lifers inside who had graduated, then recruited new inmates and convinced them to take it seriously and committed to helping other prisoners."

Kelly said that at every Kairos weekend there were maybe ten inside guys who had already made Kairos and spent the whole weekend waiting on everyone. They brought things to the table; they worked to make sure everything was functioning correctly. They were called the "inside team," and their commitment over the weekend was impressive. Kelly believed that for the Kairos program inmates to see the unbelievable sharing that the inside team offered was a profound lesson for them.

Kelly pointed out that some of the best people in Kairos were lifers in San Quentin who often had the worst possible youth conditions yet really wanted to change their lives from within, even though they were never going to be released. Kelly said, "What these lifer inmates at San Quentin had to go through to survive their parents is unbelievable. Many were screwed up psychologically and emotionally almost from the day they were born. But then they came to a realization that there was within them the power to change and to become healthy on their own. Many would call it a miracle change."

Those who had discovered hope in their lives, the hope they had lost when the bars closed behind them, became meaningful role models for the younger prisoners who were not in for such serious crimes and who would eventually be released. These older graduates really did, Kelly knew, "a wonderful job of mentoring the younger people who then realized they could improve their lives, get out, and stay out of prison once they were free again." The young inmates often reported to Kelly that Kairos and the lifer mentors were catalysts that changed their lives. Kelly told the author, "I just saw it happen, time and time again."

Although Kairos is a Christian organization, it is open to inmates of all faiths. According to Kelly, it wasn't unusual to have Muslims or Jews or followers of other faiths or no faiths attend, but "when we presented Jesus up front to that group everybody was okay with it." He had a Muslim tell him at the end of one session that he had respect for Jesus and that "I'm a better Muslim now because I made Kairos. It is the same truth."

Kelly enjoyed steady friendships with all of those incarcerated in the prison. He connected with just about every group because he knew they were all speaking the same spiritual language. Outside team members were mostly Catholic and Protestant of different denominations with various church affiliations, but that made little difference.

Of the Kairos inmates, Kelly said the Protestant church community was about two-thirds Black. The Catholic service was attended primarily by whites and Latinos with only a few Blacks in attendance, typically from Black Catholic Louisiana families. In the Kairos program, people of all races were friends and got along well.

Volunteers were typically proponents of racial equality and shared a commitment to the principles of what Jesus was about. Kelly didn't agree with all their forms of faith since some, unlike

Kelly, were Bible-thumping fundamentalists, but when they communicated in that San Quentin setting it was a "whole new world. It was just people sharing with people and showing real support and love. The effect was overwhelming."

Kairos wasn't Kelly's only San Quentin program of interest. Another one he favored was graduation day of the Prison University Project. Sponsored by Christian Patten College in the San Francisco East Bay, it brought volunteers to San Quentin to teach college courses.

Kelly recalled, "Each time there were five, ten, or fifteen inmates graduating with an AA Degree; each dressed in cap and gown and had invited their families. It was one of the most beautiful, meaningful graduations I went to. They also graduated inmates who had completed their GED and men who had earned certificates in a technical field for eventual outside employment." Kelly added, "There were maybe thirty or forty graduates at these various levels. It was a whole different experience from a graduation outside. I usually knew a third or half of those graduating."

Kelly visited not only for Kairos or special events; he often visited the Protestant chapel at 10:30 on non-Kairos Sundays and stayed for about forty-five minutes while the inmates sang. Then he walked to the Catholic chapel for the rest of the Mass, usually during the sermon. He told this author he probably had more friends in the Protestant chapel than the Catholic because more of them were Kairos graduates.

Kelly once brought his Bayside School counseling friend Dick Nelson to a Kairos final ceremony and he was amazed at the love these inmates showed for Kelly. Nelson said that all of them greeted him and talked about Kelly being a "fabulous guy."

Many inmates at San Quentin had no family or were not close to their family, so Kelly and their fellow Kairos participants became their own found family. Nelson, who called himself a "beginning Christian," told Kelly he was impressed with "what the love of the Lord had done for this class of forty-some men. Their overwhelming enthusiasm rejuvenated and inspired me spiritually."

Vic Perrella expressed that neither Kelly nor he were a "Bible thumper focused on a literal interpretation of the Bible." Perrella said, "John saw the San Quentin Kairos more as a Christian-based weekend with an intense sharing of time, energy, and love with one another. We both believed in the message of holy scripture, but focused more on the possibility of change in human behavior." He added that Kelly, "counter to the Biblical concept of original sin, had insisted that all men are intrinsically good and that everyone makes mistakes but, with the help of others, will seek changes in their lives if given the opportunity."

Patrick Kelly, John's nephew, provided this author with a window into his uncle's focus on fundamental human goodness and on restorative justice since Kelly sometimes included Patrick on his trips to San Quentin. He said, "Many inmates they encountered were like John's sons and looked to him for guidance. He was a constant in their lives and gave them an opportunity to have a dialogue about important things."

Patrick spoke to a certain inmate named Michael every time he visited. His impressions were vivid: "He was incredibly bright and charismatic. As a teenager, he was in the wrong place at the wrong time, only driving a car when a friend committed murder. Once convicted, he was locked up and the key thrown away. To society, here was a 'horrible, horrible person who could never change, a gang-banger in prison; therefore, lock him away for life.' But like most inmate friends of John's, Michael had come to terms with his crime and who he was as a person."

Patrick said he asked, "How many of us didn't do something wrong as a teenager? There are degrees of wrong, but much has to do with their youthful burst of testosterone. It seemed unfair to not give young offenders a second chance for a life." He added,, "There are some who should stay locked up like the extreme Charles Manson type but not many fit that category." Thanks to his uncle, Patrick changed how he thought about the incarcerated by meeting these "real people."

Kelly once included this author on a mid-week San Quentin visit to see firsthand not only the security and depressing confinement but also to see how the prisoners reacted to Kelly. After passing through security x-ray and the sally port cage and as we entered an open courtyard, inmates from near and far immediately gathered around him vying for attention. Kelly listened to their questions and comments treating each as a friend. We went to a conference room and listened in a town-hall type of meeting where thirty or so inmates were discussing living conditions and available self-help classes. That two-hour visit changed my perception of incarcerated felons and was worth a thousand words about the beneficial effect of Kelly's dedication to mostly Black and Latino wards of the state. Kelly was not only instrumental in Kairos, but he also volunteered in many additional San Quentin programs and especially in one focused on younger prisoners.

During one of his frequent visits to San Quentin, Kelly learned of a program designed especially for inmates serving what was called "a life sentence"—fifteen years or more to life in prison with the possibility of parole—for crimes committed before they were eighteen. In early 2011, Kelly met the nine inmates who were involved in what was known as the Kid C.A.T. (Creating Awareness Together) program. These inmates had committed serious crimes, usually murder or accessory to murder, when they were teenagers.

These now-older men had created a jailhouse curriculum to teach younger, shorter-term inmates as Kelly put it, "to wise up, and after they were released to not make the mistakes they had made." Additionally, the Kid C.A.T. volunteers were responsible for a journal and a video designed to convince at-risk teens dealing with real-life issues still outside of prison to not make their same mistakes. They also hoped to influence those working in the court system to consider better ways to deal with young offenders.

The youngest Kid C.A.T. inmate had been only fourteen when he was sentenced to state prison. He and the others were now in their early thirties; all had been in prison for at least fifteen years, and some were scheduled for a parole board hearing. According to Kelly, "The last thing we needed to do was to sentence a kid who was that age to life in an adult prison."

Kelly knew from his psychology training and from his own experience working with youth that a teenager did not have the same capacity to make decisions the way an adult did. He strongly believed that society as a whole needed to take that into account when considering the ill-advised decisions that the young person made when committing their crime. He added that the Kid C.A.T. nine, each of whom had been rehabilitated, were some of "finest human beings I had ever met in my life." Kelly loved these young men and considered them all close friends despite their backgrounds.

Brian Cahill, former Executive Director of San Francisco Catholic Charities, knew and admired Kelly's work with Samaritan House and with San Mateo youth. "But it seemed John's first love was the guys in San Quentin," he said. Cahill believed those in charge should have given Kelly a place to stay on prison grounds to cut down his travel time. "He was there on Sundays for Mass," Cahill said, "and at Protestant Chapel and to visit with the inmates. He was there Tuesday night with Vic Perrella for our Spirituality Group and there again Thursday for the Restorative Justice group. And especially he was there for Kairos on the weekends ever since they began."

Cahill said Kelly was in no way naive about the criminal records some of the men held, but Kelly respected the rehabilitation work they had undertaken, the insight and remorse they had shown, and the spiritual journey they were on. Cahill added, "No one was more affirming, less judgmental, and more supportive than John. He constantly pointed out to the inmates that in many ways, they were more evolved souls than some people on the outside."

Cahill knew Kelly's commitment to the inmates didn't stop after they were released from prison. The former priest stayed in touch with a large number of those who had been fortunate enough to gain their freedom.

Over the years, Kelly was the dedicated leader of a core group of those who conducted Kairos programs, making all but seven of forty-one programs. One absence was due to his having had the stroke in 2011, but Kelly showed his resolve and courage by surprising those he was helping by using his walker to attend his fortieth and forty-first programs. That February 2013 program was the final Kairos program he could manage physically. At that point in time, some two thousand inmates had attended the retreats Kelly had been involved in through the years.

By being part of the Kairos Organization, Kelly had joined, at the time, more than 36,000 volunteers contributing more than three million hours of service in over 400 institutions around the world. Each year, over twenty-five thousand inmates and their family members were introduced to God's love, grace, and forgiveness through that organization.

～

John Kelly eventually expanded his volunteer work beyond San Quentin. Armed with a volunteer team, he brought a quasi-Kairos weekend retreat to San Mateo County Jail inmates near where he lived.

Kelly, along with Don Zamacona, an avid Kairos participant and Redwood City Service League member, convinced County Sheriff Greg Munks to approve the idea. They put together a team of seventeen volunteers, thinking they would attract twenty or twenty-five inmates but, to their surprise, nearly seventy signed up.

On Saturday morning, August 18, 2012, Kelly, at the ripe young age of eighty-three, and his team members had entered Maguire Correctional Facility and provided Kairos-type talks to the assembled prisoners.

Team member Jerry Forbes described the initial palpable lack of trust among the inmates, recalling that they looked at the volunteers upon first meeting them as if to say, "What are you outsiders doing in here? What is in it for you? Because nobody has ever done anything for me without wanting something from me." In time, this lack of trust would be overcome.

The team spent two days in the jail, Saturday and Sunday from 8:00 a.m. to 4:30 p.m., during which they introduced restorative justice concepts encouraging prisoners to examine their lives and to consider changes. Volunteers gave short talks, but most of the program involved eliciting prisoners' input about their lives. The focus was on what changes could they make to better their lives, both in jail and when they were released.

Inmates seemed genuinely appreciative that anyone cared about them and that outsiders were offering to help them improve their current jail situation and better their lives. Kelly explained, "We learned one inmate happened to have his birthday the day we were there, so the volunteers sang happy birthday to him. Holding back tears, he told us he had never had a birthday that he could remember—no one to celebrate with at all. He said he was grateful that the team visited and spent time with his fellow inmates and him."

One "outside" team member had previously spent six years in San Quentin. He had also had a father who was a murderer and who had spent most of his adult life in prison. Moreover, his grandfather had committed a homicide and was incarcerated for many years. When this volunteer was released from prison, he made up his mind to change his life and resolved that his children would not end up in jail or prison. He told Kelly's team that he had five boys, and the next day he would be taking one of them to start college at University of California, Merced. Having "been there" behind bars at San Quentin, that volunteer gave a powerful speech that truly resonated with the county jail inmates.

At the end their visits, the prisoners, Kelly told this author, wanted to change the way they were treating people. One inmate said to him, "I think this will help me to look at my fellow inmates differently. I really want to improve my relationships with the people here."

Overall, the response at the conclusion of the retreat was "just fantastic," Kelly recalled. His volunteer friend Jerry Forbes told this author, "These inmates were really looking for something different than what caused them to be sent to jail. They had screwed up, but our object was to help them achieve insight as to what got them there and ideas about how they could avoid coming back." Forbes recalled the difference in the men—the positive change in attitude over two days—was "almost indescribable."

Having observed the prison and jail systems on a firsthand basis, Kelly told this author, "Those systems have never been geared to restoration." He had been on the governing Board of the inmate "help group" of the San Mateo County Service League and was familiar with the lack of positive assistance in the county jail.

Kelly recalled that recent jail retreat as not at all typical. In fact, it had been a real breakthrough, he believed, in terms of rehabilitation benefit. He saw the results when the volunteers visited the jail two months later and there was a distinct change of attitude among the prisoners and how they treated each other—a more positive attitude all around. Kelly, sharing his observations with this author, said:

> If our justice system can eliminate retribution and revenge and instead develop a restoring mentality, incarcerated people can immediately get well and change how their life is going. Do we want them to sit in their cells and do nothing

or do we want to help them to change? If they sit and doing absolutely nothing, we can only expect them to be released back to our neighborhoods and do the same stupid stuff all over again. Healing and restoration are what are important to avoid that revolving jail door.

Kelly knew that virtually all local jail inmates and all but a few state prison inmates were eventually released back into various communities. He acted for his own moral reasons and also for reasons of safety and the wellbeing of the public. He knew from long experience that society was best served by helping convicted felons reform before they were released.

To Kelly, restorative justice was not complicated. He recognized that crime harms people, including the criminal, and the main task of the justice systems should be to effectively repair these injuries. "Crime victims and the community also bear the brunt of crime," Kelly told this author, "and they need to be actively involved in the criminal justice process."

Kelly's spiritual and physical support of prison and jail inmates and ex inmates was frequently unpopular, but ever the strong advocate, he never took an easy path to avoid political or social pressure. He had begun his life of civil rights advocacy after twenty-five years as a Catholic priest with his decision to leave the priesthood and start a ministry for those in need. To follow his passion to help those many times forgotten, he endured mental and spiritual distress and pain by leaving a life that he had thought from his early teens would be fulfilling, only to find it was not. The result, though, of that momentous decision had been the building of Samaritan House and then the start of

John's prison ministry, legacies that those in need would benefit from and remember long into the future.

Kelly's friend Vic Perrella told this author, "Kelly truly possessed the virtue of humility and wanted no recognition; rather, he was filled with joy by helping and being of service to others." And when Perrella thought of the men who had served twenty to thirty-five years in San Quentin and were now released and out of prison, he agreed with Kelly that "there isn't a greater sense of peace and joy! Those inmates were not forgotten and they will never forget John." Perrella called Kelly the "St. Francis of Assisi of the twenty-first century" and said he had been blessed to have been part of John Kelly's life.

TEN

Sam Vaughn Success Story

WHILE WORKING WITH the "retreats" at the San Mateo County jail was rewarding, the days spent at San Quentin never left Kelly's mind. He told this author, "I received more than I gave and felt more comfortable there than even with local wealthy people who contributed to our charitable causes. The San Quentin inmates were my friends and counted on me."

A summarized version of former San Quentin inmate Sam Vaughn's story, as he told this author, reflects how Kelly befriended one of those whom he called his "long-time prison friends:"

> I was raised in the Richmond, California area. I work for the City of Richmond Office of Neighborhood Safety and we specialize in abating gun violence…. I do this work and I am passionate about it because I was one of

the problems in the community. I've lived the same life that most of these [young Richmond] folks live.

I was from a nuclear family; both parents working. I have two older sisters. We didn't have a lot but we didn't need for anything. When I was about eleven my parents split and I never understood why until I was grown. But there was drug addiction; holding grudges against one another for things done in the past. One day when I woke up in the morning for school my mom wasn't there. And she stayed gone. Then [later] she'd get into relationships which were kind of hard for me to understand.

I did really well but I would see both my parents hurting. I was eleven and my sisters were thirteen and sixteen. One got pregnant at fifteen. So, my life went from being a normal household—identified with the Cosbys...to one where I really had nothing to pull on to deal with problems in a positive way.

When the split came, I stayed with my father. I cleaned house, did his laundry, cooked dinner when he came home from work and was still getting A's and B's. I was just trying to get some kind of happiness around the household.

I'm sure my father appreciated it but it wasn't enough—he was like, 'my life sucks.' So, he was in the 'me' phase and just went bad. Both parents got really addicted to drugs, law enforcement issues, domestic issues.

I started doing what I saw. All family money went for drugs and alcohol for my parents. I stopped going to school having to wear clothes either with holes in them or too small. I did what a lot of the young men around this community do: start providing for themselves by any means necessary.

I started selling weed and crack cocaine. Then I was getting things taken from me, so now I had to have a pistol so folks didn't take what I worked for. I ended up being right smack dab in the lifestyle that these young men that we work with are in right now.

There was no peace in my heart or in my mind. I just gave up and right after my sixteenth birthday I attempted suicide and then had to deal with psychologists...but I didn't get the treatment I needed. Fortunately, I had a positive foundation because during my first ten/eleven years my father got up for work every single day and worked overtime. He at least gave me a good work ethic.

I started Job Corps where I passed a GED test and graduated earlier than if I had stayed in school. There I got a skill as a heavy equipment operator and finished Job Corps on my eighteenth birthday. I joined the union and came home waiting for work.

Home meant back to poverty, despair, old friends and old bad habits. Without money to buy drugs to sell...I attempted a robbery and wound up shooting myself. I got out of the hospital in three weeks and vowed to do something different.

I did get a job in a warehouse and, after three months, I got work in Livermore doing apprenticeship union work at eleven dollars per hour until winter came and there was no work.

I didn't yet qualify for unemployment benefits, so before I went broke, I...started selling drugs...and ended up getting into it with someone over a bad drug deal and they claimed we robbed him...and I went to jail.

In April, my employer wrote a letter saying he had a job for me and I got out on house arrest which costs about $100 per week. I brought home from work about $350 a week, minus transportation costs. I really didn't have any money but I was making it.

Unfortunately, the only place I had for house arrest was my sister's house. My sister lived with her boyfriend and his brother…who were selling crack and methamphetamine. I asked them to please just have your customers meet you around the corner…because Parole/Probation/the Police are going to come; they have the right to come in here whenever they want. They wouldn't stop selling drugs.

So, if I'm going to jail for a probation violation anyway, I might as well go back to selling drugs. Then it became very profitable. I was getting good at…making a profit, building up a great clientele. I had a supplier…and I had folks who I was supplying and was making a lot of good money.

Once you are doing well folks know and, once again, I was carrying a pistol. I got my own place. I got two cars. I was nineteen years old. I was flying off to Cabo San Lucas, New Orleans for Mardi Gras, New York for the Fourth of July. I was loving life.

Right after my twenty-first birthday we stopped at a convenience store…I saw a couple fighting and…the guy transferred his physical aggression to me. I was insecure and after having taken a couple sucker punches went and found and confronted him.

I hit him in the head with his own weapon; he wound up on life support and almost died. After some time, I turned myself in, went to trial and I was found guilty of attempted manslaughter which meant I would serve ten years in state prison.

They sent me to Corcoran Prison in Kern County, a four-hour drive from the San Francisco Bay area between Fresno and Bakersfield. It was a miserable place and I spent two years there just doing time—reading, watching movies, playing dominoes and cards, and going to chapel.

I definitely became spiritual—no, I became religious—going to chapel every Saturday thinking God would forgive me and protect me in this chaos that I'm in. And He'll reward me because I'm going to church, reading the Bible, and staying away from conflict. It really wasn't a change in mind set—just a change in actions.

I got sent to San Quentin in May of 2001 and saw all these free people (outside volunteers) and all the activities and programs they had. These outsiders came in just because they wanted to help you be a better person. And that blew my mind. You know the stigma: I'm a felon, a convict. I'm in prison so nobody trusts me; everybody thinks I'm a scumbag. I don't really deserve to have them trust me. I haven't earned it. That was my mind frame and why I got religion; I've got God and God is never going to turn His back on me.

I saw they had a college program and I thought I would have been committing another crime not to go to college. Free college—can't hurt. Plus, it got me out of the cell and homework kept me busy making my days go by quicker. It didn't hurt that there were young ladies from Berkeley, Hayward and Davis who came and taught courses. It didn't hurt to have eye candy while I was learning.

When I wasn't in school, I was in chapel and that was my life. And that's how I met John Kelly, a volunteer going to both Protestant and Catholic Chapel. John was always open and accessible and available. We talked about baseball and the things he had done in his life as a priest and now not being a priest. I was like, good for you; strong enough to make up your mind about what you truly believed.

He believed in Catholicism but had some issues with it. He believed in the freedom to worship of the Protestant Chapel yet had serious issues with that. He kind of intertwined what it took for him to be spiritual and fulfilled and just made it for himself. And that takes a strong person.

He had the strength and security to say, 'I'm going to do what I think God wants me to do and I think I am intelligent enough to figure that out on my own. I don't need somebody to tell me.' And I just loved that about him.

He encouraged me to take Kairos. And I think that honestly is when I began having a relationship with God—instead of just being religious and feeling like I was just [following] a structure to please God.

John helped me grow in a lot of ways. I was in San Quentin for six and a half years and he was there the whole time. The longer I was there the more days of the week I would see him. And he just really became a role model. That is hard to understand, since at that time he was early to mid-seventies, yet he engaged nineteen and twenty-year old gang bangers—Norteños, Sureños, Black folks from the East Bay. You could look at him as a friend; he never really had the persona of mentor. He always came as an equal which attracted people to him. But he ended up being a mentor to everyone anyway.

He just amazed me. We really got along well in there. He helped me mature as a man and grow in my spirituality and also in my mind frame. He encouraged me to get involved in activities other than just church because he understood how that can control you. He said there is more out there for your spirit than just the chapel.

With the self-help programs they were talking about your spiritual and emotional well-being and just not using God or Jesus in the wording, but it was the same concept. And that things can go wrong (spiritually) and you can still be well. That was a definite nugget that I needed. I got involved in those other things he recommended and our friendship just continued to blossom.

When I left prison, I didn't leave John. He performed my wedding, actually a renewal of vows, in February of 2011. He definitely was a part of my life, although I didn't get to hang with him the way I would want. I'd seen him a couple of times after his stroke.

John was a proud man. He hated having to be taken care of. He hated having to depend on people. He hated his walker but at least he could get around, for a while anyway. His life was to take the blows the way they came and hope your integrity and character can get you through it the best way possible.

John hadn't lost his ability to speak and that was his gift from God. He still had his mind and his ability to express what he felt and to encourage folks like me. I was glad God didn't take that from him: 'You ain't goin' to walk but I'm not going to take your speech. That is your work on this planet for Me.'

John was a ham. He didn't even need a microphone since he talked loud enough. He loved to share his God given gift. He loved singing also. In a group you could hear John above everybody else. He needed that. He had never experienced a lot of the things in life that everybody else experienced. He never experienced his own family and never experienced that attention that you would get. Every human being needs attention.

John was innately good, positive in the spirit of God. It dwelled in him on a regular basis. I don't know about when he was younger, but all the time I knew him I recognized that he was driven by the spirit...which is not true for most people. At Kelly's invitation, I spoke about restorative justice to the San Mateo Rotary group of elder, Caucasian individuals and saw how he received their respect and admiration. You can't fake it. John was just his person, his character, just who he was.

John's lack of interest in material things attracted people to him. He didn't have an income. Everything he received was a gift. Folks still viewed him as a priest and they just followed the word and took care of those [Kelly] who spiritually blessed you. He had folks pay his phone bill and car insurance and somebody who gifted the rent for his apartment. Everything that he had was because somebody wanted him to have it. He was literally like a monk living in poverty except folks didn't allow him to just live in poverty.

He was amazing. Very few people in this world have a legacy to leave. There are few people in this world who you can say their name and people would recognize it and he was definitely that person. You say his name and you will be hard pressed to find somebody who doesn't know something about him. I am grateful to have been part of John's life.

Sam Vaughn, in his Kelly-inspired mode, continues to counsel and help divert young men who cause conflict in the city of Richmond, north of Oakland, California. He and his team identify, engage, and work with trouble-prone, disadvantaged youth and mentor them one-on-one to help free them from drugs. They help these youths earn their GEDs and acquire their driver's licenses and Social Security cards to help them secure jobs and function in society. Once the young people become more stable, the volunteers help them find employment, often subsidized work, so they can wedge their foot in the door, maybe impress their employer, and continue the job unsubsidized.

Vaughn and his team have success stories to tell, but even with their guidance and help from family and friends "street code," many times involving gangs, still gets in their way. But he learned from Kelly not to give up. So he and his team keep focusing on the troubled youth, knowing that success is not just keeping these youth from pulling the trigger or making another foolish mistake, but helping these young men to be functional, law-abiding citizens. This would mean a safer Richmond and a safer world for all.

ELEVEN

Reforming Criminal Justice

THROUGHOUT HIS LIFE, John Kelly railed against what he saw as an unfair politically influenced criminal justice system that often abused and punished rather than rehabilitated both criminals and their victims. He continually lobbied for systemic reform, and as a man of action, not just words, he took his fight to those in power.

Always focused on San Quentin lifer inmates, some sentenced while still in their teens, Kelly and others successfully advocated for California State Senate bill SB 9. This law would allow inmates who were juveniles when they committed their crimes to petition judges, through an attorney or on their own, for reconsideration of their sentences after they had served at least fifteen years in prison. This bill eventually passed the legislature and was signed into law by Governor Jerry Brown on September 30, 2012.

The new law allowed judges the discretion to reduce even a life sentence with no possibility of parole to twenty-five years to life with the possibility of parole if the inmate showed remorse and had taken steps toward rehabilitation. It was an important reform, to be sure, but according to Kelly, it was only a small step considering the pervasive need for criminal justice reform and the vast populations incarcerated in California and other U.S. prisons.

In 1980, Kelly knew California had twelve prisons containing twenty thousand inmates, and by 2010, there were thirty-three prisons housing one hundred seventy thousand inmates. The state sent some nonviolent prisoners back to county jails, and by 2017, the court-ordered prison population had been reduced to around one hundred fifteen thousand. Still, virtually all California's thirty-five prison facilities were above 100 percent rated capacity. At the time, Kelly was justifiably troubled, not just by the overcrowding but because Black prisoners represented 28 percent of the inmates while only being 6 percent of the state's population.

Kelly, ever caring about those incarcerated, had another strong concern, this one dealing with the lobbying power of the prison guard union and its determination to keep prisons full of inmates to preserve jobs. He told this author "that the guards' union was always influential and effective in protecting their vested interests."

For instance, in 2014, Kelly knew about eight thousand California prison guards (or one-third the number of guards in the state) made over $100,000 per year total wages including overtime, and they could retire at age fifty-five with 85 percent of their salary. If prison populations were to be further reduced, there would be fewer jobs for guards and those jobs might not pay as much. "That factor was a driving force whether we liked it or not," he said.

Regarding his views on reducing prison populations, Kelly added, "We have to have more input from prison leadership and staff capable of determining whether a prisoner will be a danger to society or if instead they've reached the point of rehabilitation where they can be a plus to society." Kelly believed that a prisoner about to be released would already have shown signs indicating whether he would make it on the outside or return to a life of crime. Kelly added, "It's about how they have been conducting their lives inside prison. Have they really been committed to helping other people including fellow inmates? What kind of programs have they been involved in? Did they become better educated? Did they take advantage of training to be effective when they were going to be released? These are real clues that need to be considered."

Kelly believed lifers were unique in terms of recidivism: "They had been locked up for twenty or more years and they had either vegetated or (hopefully) they'd wised up and changed." At the time, California Department of Corrections officials conducted a study of lifers who were paroled between 1990 and 2010. According to Kelly, "There were 988 who were paroled and only thirteen re-offended and none of them for serious crimes."

However, Kelly knew, a lifer's prospect of actually being granted parole by the Board of Parole Hearings and not having the decision reversed by the governor was slim. From 1991 to 2010, that possibility of parole had ranged between 0 and 7 percent.

During his lifetime, Kelly maintained that many of those in prison had changed their lives: "They are redeemed people. I certainly feel for their victims and their families, but society had not accepted that forgiveness was possible and important. There hadn't been a willingness to accept that criminals could reform and be an asset to their families and society." Kelly said that he had met "some genuine and caring men in prison. They had completely changed their outlooks and lives. Not all, of course, but we needed a better system of evaluating prisoners for parole and release back into society."

Kelly recalled driving home once after meeting with the nine Kid C.A.T. prisoners who had committed crimes as teens. Asked by some friends if he was crazy for respecting those inmates as human beings even though they did horrible things, he replied that he did respect them and hoped people were becoming aware that the prisoners themselves had often been victimized. He told this author, "It is difficult to understand what horrors some of these men went through growing up trying to survive. One of them in my meeting group said he had nine different 'fathers.' His mother was all over the place. He had no stability whatsoever growing up. Some of the stepfathers beat him. By the time he was fifteen years old, he'd gone through pure unadulterated hell."

Kelly went on to tell a story about an inmate who grew up in an atmosphere that caused him to develop a mountain of rage inside. "As a little kid with no power," Kelly recalled, "he didn't know what to do with his anger—how to get it out of his system. 'Who was there to help him?' I wondered."

At the end of this young man's Kairos weekend, he realized he had used his pent-up anger to hurt people. This inmate knew he had hurt himself more than anybody else had and that things needed to change. Kelly shared these inmates' stories with people who had led a relatively normal life, he said, but "they couldn't understand what it was like to grow up that way. They couldn't appreciate the real torment some of these prisoners have had to survive. Yet many of those prisoners were able, with help like from Kairos, to rehabilitate themselves."

Restoring Justice

John Kelly, based on his extensive experience with the application and results of criminal law, was concerned about the pervasive focus on punishment. He told this author, "Criminal justice, as we now have it—somebody commits an offense and the whole purpose of how the State deals with it is, 'How serious is it? How much (prison) time do we have to give the offender?' And if there are victims, the State's only purpose has been to determine the seriousness of the offense and to know what happened to them solely to determine sentencing (and not to help heal the victims)."

Kelly pointed out the huge difference between the accused who could afford a private lawyer and the poor, mainly Black and Latino, who received a court appointed defense lawyer since the outcome typically favored those with high-paid legal help. Also, he saw a huge difference between how the courts handled things in wealthy urban areas compared to the poor rural east side of the state in the California Central Valley. Regarding the poorer areas, he said, "Forget it—the defendant gets clobbered. It is a whole different ball game. What can we do to ensure more equal defense representation?" [Author's note: In 2013, the report of the Sentencing Project to the UN Human Rights Committee concluded that "the United States in effect operates two distinct criminal justice systems; one for wealthy people and another for poor people and minorities."]

Kelly's concept of restorative justice was simple: "A crime is a failure in how the community should function. Something goes wrong and there is a breakdown in relationships among people." To deal with this breakdown, he said, "The government entity should be directed to two key things: healing and restoration.

But in the current criminal justice system, those are not the priorities."

Kelly often touted San Quentin as unique among California prisons in that it provided numerous rehabilitation programs. Kelly attended a graduation ceremony every year where he was told once by the official in charge that there were about three thousand people who visited San Quentin every month to help inmates who wanted to help themselves. The official showed Kelly a thirteen-page list of the kind of self-help programs that were available inside San Quentin. Kelly regularly volunteered in many of those programs.

Kelly described one of his typical weeks at San Quentin: "Tuesday night we had a group called 'Spirituality.' Sixteen inmates and four outsiders discussed, 'How can I change my life?' or 'How do I find some peace in my life?' Past topics had been 'How to deal with anger,' 'Empathy,' and 'How to forgive.'"

Kelly wished he could record some of the comments made by the inmates (this was not allowed) as the discussion went around the table. "These inmates came back to participate every Tuesday night, week after week," he said.

One Thursday after a scheduled noon speech to the San Mateo Rotary, Kelly traveled the nearly forty miles to San Quentin for an evening session on restorative justice. This group had been ongoing for seven years, and Kelly had been there from the beginning. He told this author that on this particular night, there were seventy inmates discussing elements of restorative justice. They were taking responsibility, he noted, for "what I did; being aware of all the people I hurt; finding some way that I can possibly make their life better; being aware of all the victims that were in my life. They then asked themselves and they asked their cohorts what they personally could do to change the conditions and atmosphere in their communities so crime wouldn't continue."

The State of California was "horrible in the way it treated victims," Kelly believed. "They do not take into consideration the trauma or the need for victim rehabilitation." He noted that the Victims' Rights Office of the State of California was in the same Sacramento office building as the Department of Corrections and Rehabilitation. He believed that collaboration and close association was not an accident; that the co-location favored corrections and retribution rather than rehabilitation, bowing to the political pressures of the times.

Kelly told this author he had had many encounters with and was particularly disturbed by the California Board of Parole Hearings. He believed the overall system was unfair and its effect on victims was unfortunate. "When the Board doesn't want to make their own difficult decision, they have an En Banc [before the whole] Board hearing where non-board members and the general public could testify in favor of or against an inmate." He sat through three or four of these hearings and was saddened to see a victim testify, now twenty-five years after the crime was committed, spouting out venom against the criminal. The victim's need for retribution and revenge actually had helped destroy their own life in the process. Kelly called for "a better way to really help crime victims."

Kelly, in public appearances, made a strong case that inmates were also victims. He cited a friend who spent time at San Quentin and after his release did "fabulous work in the community." His ex-con friend's early life story, Kelly said, "blew me out of the water. When he was born, his father was in prison and his mother was a drug addict. I wondered, 'How could this guy survive his upbringing? And how do we break this cycle of poverty and crime?'"

Kelly believed that an important element of restorative justice was helping ex-cons readjust to life outside of prison. Of Kelly's friends who had been released, most had served twenty to twenty-five years, and one served thirty-two years. Some had spent more time inside than outside of prison, and when they were released, the world was not the same as it had been before they were imprisoned. Children were grown, maybe married with children and grandchildren, and the prisoner's parents may very well have died. Their neighborhood would be changed or maybe no longer even exist. Virtually nothing would be the same as when they began their sentence so many years ago.

Kelly invested considerable time and energy into helping released prisoners reconnect with their communities and especially with their families. He knew, though, that sometimes their family was the problem in the first place, and he therefore stressed the importance of prison administration finding out before a prisoner was released if the prisoner would be able to successfully rejoin their family or not.

Kelly said that the prison location assigned to an inmate could affect their ability to keep even functional families together. If someone was convicted of a crime in San Diego, he may be sent to San Quentin in northern California or if convicted in the north, sent south. Maintaining family connection under those conditions was especially challenging. Many prisoners lost their family connections and had to start over after they were released. As convicted felons without a ready support network, they would have an even more difficult time integrating back into society.

One restorative justice goal Kelly supported was to create more transitional housing to help prisoners when they were released. One such place in Oakland was called Options and was where many ex-inmates ended up. They were required to reside there for a period of time and were given a chance to get reacquainted with the community. Kelly told this author, "There is a desperate need for more of this to happen because these men are otherwise left out to dry in a lot of ways. That was a question for many communities: are they willing to develop facilities for the released prisoners to spend some transition time?"

At the San Mateo County Service League, they had developed over recent years five- and six-unit locations in Redwood City that provided a transition for women. Kelly often coordinated with them helping to find housing and jobs for men and women released from jail and insisted, "We need more and more of that kind of thing."

STUDENT LECTURE

John Kelly often spoke to community groups as an advocate of criminal justice reform. At one point, he addressed Jennifer Kammeyer's Leadership Communications class and Dr. Karen Lovaas' Rhetoric of Criminality and Punishment class at San Francisco State University.

In this lecture, he said, "One of the major disasters in the last twenty or thirty years in California has been the criminal justice system." He described to these two classes his proposed solution to fix the disaster as being restorative justice. He went on to define it as "Number one, the offender: What did he do? Whom did he hurt? Number two: How do we take care of victims whose lives get disrupted in a major way? And number three: How do we change our communities so all this horrible stuff doesn't keep happening?"

Believing young people would be the future social change agents to reduce crime in their communities, Kelly challenged the students to imagine if the California Department of Corrections and Rehabilitations changed its focus. He stated, "What if the minute somebody was arrested for a crime, the authorities tried to make the person arrested well instead of focusing *only* on how much jail or prison time they needed to ensure they did not commit another crime? The results could be amazing."

Kelly acknowledged to the students that the inmates had done some "pretty horrible things." But he was also aware, he said, of the "unbelievable ability of human beings to change." He described a year-long "Victims and Offenders Education Program where every inmate was challenged to clearly under-stand what he did and thoroughly understand the people he hurt—not only the victims, but the inmate's own family and community.

As the college class watched and listened in earnest, Kelly told them that as part of that program, "The prisoner then writes a letter to their victim that doesn't necessarily get sent. The point is that the offender writes about his awareness of the seriousness of what he did."

As an aside, Kelly added that, "Prison lifers characteristically tended to be way ahead of the short-termers when it came to facing the impact of their crimes and to change. Many are thoroughly committed to find a way to impact the outside world and make sure that young people didn't end up making the same mistakes they did."

Kelly told the students there was also an exceptional Solano State Prison certification program called Alternatives to Violence that trained about forty inmates to counsel other inmates. As part of the Solano program, ex-con training leader James Alexander lectured to the current state prison inmates. Kelly had attended Alexander's talk and was amazed at how afterwards the current prisoners said "hello, smiled, and thanked Alexander for all that his counsel had done for them."

Kelly went on to tell the San Francisco State students about San Jose journalist John Hubner, who had written the book *Last Chance in Texas*. Hubner watched and chronicled the rehabilitation process in the Giddings State School, home to "the worst of the worst" juveniles incarcerated in Texas. There, Hubner reported, every kid had to write the story of his life. Other kids then acted out all the characters in the kid's story in front of him. In most cases, the serious damage they had done dawned on the youth and it helped them change. Sadly, if the young inmate could not understand the depth of what he did and show some empathy, the administration decided he was so far gone that he could not be rehabilitated.

Kelly told the students, too, about a young man recently released from the old San Mateo County Maguire jail. He hadn't committed a crime before, but happened to be hanging around with some bad influences. They burglarized a house with this young man as the driver.

A conviction followed and he spent six months in the county jail. Kelly raised his voice when he said that while the youngster was incarcerated, he did "absolutely nothing, just sat there—a total waste of time. We should have used restorative justice to rehabilitate this first-time offender and had some way to change his thinking without necessarily even having to put him in jail to do it." Ever the optimist, Kelly said, "It's possible; it can happen."

Kelly gave another example of a young man from his self-help group in San Quentin who was "released on parole, found a lady friend with a little boy, and began living together out in the country on a farm. His parole officer came by and found the boy's BB gun and violated him [wrote him up] for breaking parole. He was sent back to San Quentin and thrown into a prison area called West Block for six months doing absolutely nothing. They finally released him, but for this ex-con, it was another total waste of time and energy."

Kelly went on to describe how the "tough-on-crime" movement had become more popular, beginning in the mid-1970s and up to around 2010. He knew that the State of California had passed what he called "some of the most insane initiatives" to make it increasingly difficult for people caught up in crime to ever become rehabilitated. Then in his first term, Governor Jerry

Brown, responding to that overwhelming movement, committed what Kelly believed to be "a very disastrous mistake." He signed into law Senate Bill 42 in 1976 which changed the criminal sentencing process from indeterminate to determinate. [Author's note: Brown served as the thirty-fourth governor of California from 1975 to 1983 and again as the thirty-ninth governor from 2011 to 2019. In between those terms, he was California Attorney General from 2007 to 2011.]

Before this law was passed, Kelly knew if someone was in prison with a typically indeterminate sentence, he or she didn't necessarily have to serve their maximum sentence. Instead, they could reform and be eligible for release for good behavior after their legally required minimum sentence. Governor Brown's determinate sentencing initiative acted to fix an end date to an inmate's sentence. As a result, many inmates decided that they were not going to work very hard at reforming themselves because they were stuck in prison until their fixed end date—so why bother? That made a huge difference in their attitude, Kelly believed. That change, in addition to initiatives like the "Three Strikes" (i.e. three convictions and life imprisonment) initiative, according to Kelly "were absolutely absurd." Due to 2011 legislation and the 2016 passage of Governor Brown-sponsored statewide proposition 57, California moved away from determinate sentencing to a less harsh approach that recreated incentive for inmates to reform. Kelly had cheered the decision.

Once again, Kelly explained, a "lifer" could be sentenced to fifteen or more years to life in prison, but with good behavior he would be eligible for parole at the end of the fifteen-year minimum. Unfortunately, Kelly said, the tough-on-crime political environment persisted in the criminal justice system. He knew of no "lifer" who had served only his minimum time; most were not released until three, four, or ten years past their original minimum sentence.

Once a "lifer" had served his minimum time, he had the right to appeal to the Board of Parole Hearings to have them decide if he was suitable to be released. But in practice, fewer than 10 percent of inmates even received a hearing. Kelly said, "First, three Board of Parole members visit a prison to interview an inmate and decide if he is suitable for release; their recommendations were forwarded to the whole Board for a final decision." Many times, then, no hearing was ever held; any chance of release ended right then.

The Board of Parole Hearings membership was a governor-appointed body, and as long as Kelly had been involved, "everybody on the Board had had a criminal justice background—even though State law specified that the Board composition should be a mixed group across California society." This was a mistake, Kelly believed, and an unfair one. [Author's note: The board is substantially more diverse in 2021 due to former Governor Brown appointments.]

Kelly told the attentive students that back in 1988, the state had passed statewide ballot Proposition 89, which provided that even after the Board of Parole Hearings gave an approval, the governor would have thirty days to decide if he wanted to accept or deny their decision.

Kelly, never one to hold back a strong opinion, then described Governor Pete Wilson as "horrible," approving only 5 percent of the Parole Board approval recommendations. Kelly then attacked the performance of the next governor, Gray Davis, stating that it was "absolutely abominable his having said, 'I will never let a lifer out while I am governor.'" From 1999 to 2003, Kelly knew, Davis had reviewed 371 parole grants and only approved nine. His replacement, Governor Arnold Schwarzenegger, had approved about 30 percent of parole recommendations.

Next up was the second of Jerry Brown's terms as governor, and according to the Crime Victims Action Alliance, during his term from 2011 to 2019, he approved 85 to 90 percent of Board recommendations. Kelly praised Governor Brown for his admirable record of accepting parole recommendations, believing these decisions largely offset his earlier "mistaken" advocacy of determinate sentencing enacted during his first term.

Recounting action he had taken to learn about the judicial and appeal process, Kelly told the student group that he had attended the En Banc hearing of James Alexander in Sacramento where fifteen citizens testified that he "was one of the finest human beings they had ever met." But a district attorney's office representative from San Diego gave a vigorous condemnation of Alexander, and he was turned down for parole. Fortunately, that decision was reversed when a judge decided that the board had treated him unjustly and that he should be released.

Kelly further told the students that he once had received a letter from a private citizen who wrote that his son-in-law had been murdered on the street in Palo Alto by a gang of Tongans who were now all incarcerated in San Quentin. The writer asked Kelly to look up the Tongan inmates, tell them the family was not angry with them, and tell them that they should simply change and succeed in becoming well. Kelly treasured that letter and considered it one of the most powerful restorative justice examples he had ever received. He told this author, "I think that sort of forgiveness shows real courage. I had never seen anything more moving than to see an offender and a victim sharing together what they have both experienced in trying to reach restoration. It can happen."

Another San Quentin program Kelly described to the students was called "Malachi Dads." It was designed to help inmates become better dads and teach them how they could best fulfill their role as a parent. For many incarcerated inmates, the real tragedy of their lives was that they were unable to be the parents that they ought to have been.

Kelly completed his lecture by reciting the pledge that the inmates recited after every Thursday evening session at San Quentin Prison called the "Restorative Justice Pledge:"

- I believe that violence is not a solution to any problem.
- I believe that every person is endowed with a sacred dignity.
- I believe that every person is capable of changing, healing, and being restored.
- I pledge to respect the dignity of every person.
- I pledge to overcome violence with love and compassion.
- I pledge to accompany and support anyone affected by crime on their healing journey.
- I pledge to be an instrument of restoration, forgiveness, and reconciliation.

TWELVE

James Alexander Success Story

JAMES ALEXANDER, ALEX, mentioned earlier, grew up in the infamous southside Chicago redevelopment projects raised by alcoholic parents. Because of his high elementary school grades, he was selected to attend the highly-rated Lane Tech College Prep High School in Chicago's north side. While there, the Black, pudgy, previously unpopular Alexander unexpectedly received an invitation to a white "in-crowd" party in a well-to-do suburb near the school. He accepted and attended the across-town gathering against his mother's vehement wishes.

While taking the EL train home late that night, he was mugged, stabbed, thrown off the station platform, and left for dead in the mid-winter snow. Found near death early the following morning and rushed to the hospital, he was saved but found to be partially paralyzed. Slowly and painfully, he recovered the use of his body, relearned to walk, and endured a many-month rehabilitation. His lost academic year required an unfortunate switch from Lane Tech to what he called a "disaster" local high school where he was given a tattered textbook like the one he had read two years before at Lane.

His new schoolteachers were all in "survival mode" and unable to maintain class discipline. He dropped out after a semester "because there was not much learning going on there." Summarized, here is Alexander's telling of his story from age seventeen when, with his mother's reluctant permission, he joined the Marines, stumbled into criminal trouble, and met John Kelly in prison:

> I went into the Marine Corps at 185 pounds and three months later I came out 135 pounds. They worked my butt off. They did everything they could to get me to drop out. But it was my last chance, my last hope; there was no way I was going to drop out. The boot-camp drill instructors called me a chocolate Pillsbury Dough Boy. At the graduation ceremony a drill instructor said, 'Won't your mother be proud of you.'

> I served in Okinawa, the Philippines, Thailand, and Korea for about a year. Came back Stateside to Camp Pendleton, California where my older brother was stationed with his wife. Her brother also was a Marine who lived off base with his girlfriend and unknown to me was about to get kicked out of the Marine Corps for dealing drugs. He befriended me and I was just happy that someone wanted to be my friend.

Months later…he said he needed my help on a drug deal gone bad. I agreed and went with him and his friends to a drug dealer's apartment. I was the youngest, shortest guy that they gave the gun to. I lifted and pointed the weapon not knowing it had a 'hair trigger,' it discharged and so in March of 1983 I took a man's life.

Following his arrest, trial, and mistrial, Alexander was again tried by a jury, convicted of second-degree murder, and sentenced to fifteen years to life at Soledad Prison 130 miles south of San Francisco. Because he was considered a Soledad troublemaker, his punishment was a transfer to high-security, death-row, isolation hold at San Quentin State Prison north of San Francisco. As told to this author, there he encountered his saving grace:

I met John Kelly in October of 1995 as part of the Kairos Program, the three-day Christian based workshop. It was extraordinary because there was a group of (mostly Black) prisoners who were meeting these (mostly white) guys who came in from free society. From the get-go, we were treated as though we were human beings, not prisoners. They looked past the prison blue denim uniform and they saw souls.

I was struck immediately because John Kelly was a tall figure and had that deep voice. He commanded attention just by his presence. I was fortunate enough to be at John's table in the San

Quentin prison retreat. We talked and I was impressed immediately, not just by his presence but by his sincerity. We connected immediately. After that weekend I continued to be part of Kairos 'inside.' When they would have other weekends, I would volunteer to serve. I became a part of the Kairos family at San Quentin.

But something happened, say six or seven months later. I ran into a bit of difficulty inside the prison. I began to question my faith; I had pretty much given up on the church because of a disagreement with a fellow Christian. I did not know how to resolve it so I stayed away. John Kelly, having not seen me around, inquired about me. I was kind of isolating myself. I was becoming a bit of a loner.

I had been walking alone around the lower recreation yard circular track of San Quentin prison; only a few inmates were out because of the rain. Having been sentenced to a life term in prison, I didn't think many people cared about me. I had pretty much given up after twelve years.

I saw these two figures in the distance, one tall and the other shorter, out walking in the rain. As I got closer, I recognized the taller guy and it was John Kelly. I asked, 'What are you doing out here? And he says, "Looking for you." He says,

"Alex, where have you been?"' I was just blown away by the fact that he would come down and look for me.

We talked and it helped me get past my feelings of depression. He helped me get back into the Church. He helped me to reclaim some of the relationships I had walked away from—some of the people who had had an interest in me. He saved my life. I hope that doesn't sound too over dramatic. I might have been one of the…. Who knows? I don't want to even think about it.

He helped me so much. He said he wanted me to get involved in other programs too. They had a Toastmasters speaking program and he said, "'Do it." I said, "I'm so shy. I can't get in front of people. I hear my Chicago accent and think, what is this guy talking about? No, go for it."' And I did. I got involved with Toastmasters, gave my first speech in front of twenty or thirty people…with buckets of perspiration coming off my head. I got through it, survived, kept going and I got better. They made me president of the club about a year later. That's the kind of effect John Kelly had on me. Had he not suggested that I could do it, get involved, I would not even have thought about it. He believed in me and that is huge, that is huge.

In 2001, I got shipped off from San Quentin to Old Folsom Prison twenty miles northeast of Sacramento. John Kelly found me; he is always finding me. *[big smile]*. I was in the midst of depression. John would write support letters for my parole hearings. John's letters were very well written, but the parole commission still said no. But one of our Kairos outside brothers, Eugene Kirkham and his wife Cody, would come and visit in Old Folsom.

I think around 2002, they asked, 'Why aren't you getting out?' In 2004 Eugene got his California Bar license renewed and in 2006 for my parole hearing he was going to be my attorney. The Board did sign off and found me suitable for parole but Governor Schwarzenegger said no. In 2007 the Board again found me suitable but the same governor again said no. Same story in 2008, when a three-year minimum before returning for another hearing had been instituted.

After the 2008 turn down I wanted to give up but John Kelly and Kairos team helper Pat Tubman and her husband said that you have to find something; you can't just give up. I didn't know if I could do three more years. I was in so much pain that I didn't know what to do with myself.

I started a California Coast University College correspondence course with some encouragement from John. I got my first A in my first course; I thought, I can do this. Pat Tubman and her husband were putting up money and other supporters paid for legal costs. So, I can do no less than the best I can do. If I can get an A on the first course then I can get an A on the next one and I did. [In January of 2012, James graduated with a Bachelor of Science degree in Psychology—summa cum laude.]

John Kelly and some of my other supporters went to Sacramento to appeal on my behalf in 2009-2010 in front of the full Parole Board. I couldn't be there and, in any case, it didn't turn out well. The governor would not relent. In early 2011, I went to the Board and again they found me suitable for parole.

We were all set to wait five months to validate the finding by the new Governor, Jerry Brown. But the California Court of Appeals upheld a second order that I be released. I was in prison for twenty-eight years from March of 1983 to April of 2011 and paroled technically for life, but unofficially after five years you could be released.

Gene, with his wife Katrina and former wife Cody, were waiting for me in Santa Rosa. I had on these old sweat clothes but they took me to a nice restaurant in Calistoga where I ate halibut which I had dreamed about. They said, come to work for us at the winery; we'll find something for you to do.

I was interviewed in 2013 by Sonoma County Alcohol and Drugs Services to be an alcohol and drug service counselor. I applied for my California Association of Alcohol and Drug Abuse Counselor license. I've done the written examination and I need a certain number of counseling hours to get the license. I have the credentials and the degree and out of seventy-three applicants my standing was sixth.

Alexander secured an "on call" alcohol and drug counseling job in St. Helena, Napa County and is working part-time, extra-help with Sonoma County as well.

John Kelly is the number one reason that I am sitting here today. If it hadn't been for the impact Kelly had on my life, I wouldn't be talking to you today. This man has assisted me far beyond what is called for. We've got this personal relationship. I mean he's helped me like I was his son. He's been there for me. I talk to him once a week. I am so grateful to him and glad to have his presence in my life, his spirit in my life. He is a great father to have—Father Kelly.

James Alexander, raised in poverty by a dysfunctional mother and stepfather, had a biological father who failed to participate in his life. High school was a social, then academic, disaster, so his only option was to join the Marines, where he learned discipline and started in a responsible adult direction. Unfortunately, he stumbled back into the troubled environment he thought he had left behind, was caught in a drug deal gone bad, convicted, and sentenced to a potential wasted life in prison. By great good fortune in San Quentin Prison after he had lost all hope, John Kelly rescued him and became his "Father Kelly" who treated him like his own son. Alexander married and now works full time as a counselor north of San Francisco. James Alexander's August 15, 2019 autobiography *Courage in the Face of Cruelty...* is available at Amazon.com.

Kelly and San Quentin "Buddies."

Kelly in the San Quentin center courtyard.

John Kelly, James Alexander, and benefac-
tor Pat Tubman—CA Solano Prison.

THIRTEEN

Thoughts on Religion

KELLY, PHYSICALLY ACTIVE his whole life, had been inca-pacitated by his stroke and eventually bedridden, mak-ing the last two years of his life difficult. It was, however, an opportunity for us to become friends and to learn much about what made him tick. For the price of a medium chai latte and a bear claw pastry (and a bagel for Tiki, his Tongan caretaker) he gladly visited with me from about 8:30 to 9:15 every Monday morning for most of the two years. Five minutes late and he groused, "I thought you weren't coming." After he had been con-vinced to reinstall his one functioning hearing aid and turn down his loud classic music station, we would talk about local, national, and world events, spirituality, and what might come next.

Ever thoughtful and curious, Kelly shared many of his ideas and conclusions about religion as he neared the end of his life, providing a window into his spiritual mindset. First as a seminarian, then living the roles of parish priest and Catholic high school teacher, he had learned and accepted the traditional Catholic Church understanding of Jesus from Catholic literature and liturgy.

But increasingly over the years, Kelly could not reconcile his Jesus image with Christian—specifically Catholic Church—activity in his real world. For his subsequent thirty-three non-priest years, he continually reexamined who Jesus was to him and how he wanted to live his life as social justice became his driving force. Certainly, his views may conflict and even upset some traditional Catholics, but Kelly was a man of purpose—a strong advocate for his own beliefs.

What follows offers insight into Kelly's views on many "religious" subjects:

After much thought and reasoning, Kelly ultimately believed that Jesus was a "good person, thoroughly evolved as a human being, thoroughly God-oriented." Kelly said he came to believe "that when the world became too confusing with evil dominating, God sends someone like Jesus or Krishna or Mohammad to set the planet back on a spiritual path." Kelly believed that Jesus was a "God force prophet" sent on such a mission.

The former priest once rhetorically asked, "If Jesus is so obviously *the* son of God and the *only* one who brought truth into the world, why hasn't he caught on in other parts of the world? What was going on in those other areas to replace what we believe Jesus was?" Kelly ultimately concluded that Jesus arrived 2,000 years ago to bring to his people spiritual awareness regarding their particular time and place and the ability, if they could grasp it, to spread his message to other times and places.

Kelly believed life lessons were similar in many spiritual practices and that "every human being walking the face of the earth has the potential to become self-realized, that is to reach full human potential, and has the *responsibility* to become self-realized." Many prophets, gurus, and avatars have brought us understanding about how we go about doing that.

Kelly had been introduced to Eastern spirituality through the publications of the Himalayan Institute. Like Catholic spiritual guru Thomas Merton, Kelly had been open to other religions and spiritualities despite Catholic dogma that restricted such beliefs. What Kelly learned from his readings were the eight limbs (suggestion steps, not the popularized posture exercises) of Yoga to bring personal awareness, liberation, and peace without structured religion. Having grown dissatisfied with organized religion as he perceived it, Kelly found the Himalayan Institute approach "profoundly spiritual and realistic." He began to learn about arriving at liberation and self-awareness through means other than Christianity.

To explore these Eastern and Hindu beliefs and worship, Kelly decided in his only trip outside the United States to attend the January 2001 world-renowned Maha Kumbh Mela in Allahabad [now Prayagraj], India. During this pilgrimage, he would gain the "full knowledge of what it meant to be a human being and to be connected with the God force totally in every phase and moment of your existence."

Kelly's group flew from San Francisco to Hong Kong to Singapore and then to New Delhi, India. He remembered the New Delhi airport being filled with homeless people sleeping on the floor. He recalled, "It was cluttered and dirty." On the ten-hour train ride to Allahabad, Kelly remembered his surprise when he saw the little sign that warned not to use the commodes in the stations since they emptied right onto the tracks. "Their culture was totally different from ours," he told this author.

Kelly and nearly two hundred Westerners attending this Institute pilgrimage resided in tents overlooking the Ganges River. Small in-house celebrations were held by the trip organizers, and occasionally members of the group would walk down to the Ganges and join larger celebrations. Kelly remembered being fascinated at in-house sessions where Indian gurus described their lives and their hopes for India to reach a balance between Eastern spirituality and Western technology. They expressed hope "that our cultures would help each other out." He certainly agreed.

The Dalai Lama passed a few feet from awestruck Kelly in a large main tent to make his "very impressive presentation." Everyone had respectfully removed their shoes before entering the tent, and after the presentation, they exited. In the scramble for shoes, Kelly's were gone. Fortunately, Kelly had spare shoes back at his tent.

At one point, Kelly's group took a boat ride into the central area when he recalled passing a dead body in the water and again marveled at the cultural differences between home and India. January twenty-fourth was the main celebration day, and the big devotional-act ritual was a dip in the Ganges. "I did get out of the boat into and out of the water fast," he recalled. "When I came home to the U.S., something about the exposure to that river water caused all the skin to peel off the bottom of my feet."

Kelly concluded during his trip that India "had this great history of spirituality, but through the caste system, they separated humanity into sections, and it was pretty hard to cross over." He feared that even if India continued to technologically advance, it would benefit very few—that already, India's economic growth had been confined to small parts of the country and "that the poor were not going to get anything out of it."

The saddest and most frustrating aspect of India Kelly witnessed dealt with a two-hour bus ride to the spiritual town of Varanasi. Going through small towns, "on one side of the bus you'd see all these kids dressed 'to the nines' going to school—a lot of the schools are run by the Christian missionaries. Around on the other side of the bus sitting by the roadside were the 'Untouchable' kids in rags who weren't allowed to go to school. That whole 'Untouchable' thing was horrible to see in action."

Kelly reflected that listening to the Indian gurus was somewhat like hearing Bible stories and that the seminar message was "exactly the same message as what Jesus said." Since Jesus had no multi-media and there was then little communication among parts of the world, he concluded that "this God force brought His message through different prophets in different formats to different parts of the world at different times." Kelly considered all forms of holy scripture, including the Bible, as "not literally what happened. The message came through the story; Jesus, for example, spoke in parables as the best way to convey his message."

Most of all, Kelly uncovered for himself, during the trip and from all his reading, alternate spiritual choices. He noted that "other people in history and other cultures have discovered this same God force in different ways." One book he studied nearly as much as the Gospels after his pilgrimage was *Abhinavagupta's Commentary on the Bhagavad Gita*. Another book was *How to Know God* [Swami Prabhavananda], which he maintained was "based on the full understanding of all eight steps of Yoga, not just the exercises."

Well into his later years, Kelly continued to read the Bible, especially the gospel of John, and according to those readings, he concluded that "Jesus, during his brief public life, had a horrible time getting anyone to understand who he was. Sure, he created a lot of energy and excitement, but there were not many people who really grasped what he was about. Jesus saw what had been going wrong with Judaism in his day and saw what didn't work; he started making people think differently."

Kelly was certain the foundational Christian belief that Jesus died for our sins made no sense to him—"As if there were a God who demanded redeeming. Jesus as a Jew was not interested in starting a new religion but only reforming the commonly known abuses of Judaism. They totally didn't get what Jesus was all about."

Kelly came to believe that almost every day of the three years of Jesus' public life, he was attempting to educate the populace, but behind the friendly crowds were men called Scribes and Pharisees. Kelly proposed that these "hecklers continuously tried to show that Jesus didn't know what he was talking about. Jesus went through hell and had to retreat to solitude every day to put himself back together based on all the crap he had to endure."

Based on his readings and thought process, Kelly described Jesus as a "political rabble rouser" and thought his disruption of the temple money changers might have been the final straw. The political/religious leadership knew then he had to go. He was a "threat to their privileged leadership and they had to get rid of him because their power base was being overthrown."

Kelly associated the corrupt Jewish Pharisee environment during Jesus' time with the Catholic Church's failure to focus on social justice and "why I could not be a priest anymore."

From his perspective, he said, "Church liturgy was all window dressing and looking good. It was having people singing and getting all excited and then going home and forgetting everything. Modern Christians often saw Jesus as a mythological figure, not a real person."

Often, Kelly admitted, when he attended San Quentin Sunday Mass, he redid the wording of the Catholic liturgy in his head "because it didn't fit with who I was. The Mass language was archaic, non-growth oriented, and not relative to present reality. It once had a purpose for Jesus and his twelve last supper buddies, but not anymore."

Rather than believe that Jesus died for our sins, Kelly instead believed that "the God who put this universe together built in potential for growth and development and trusted human beings to make it happen." He lamented that "one of the sneaky ways we cop out is to say that Jesus is it, once and for all, and nothing is ever going to change." He added, "That's what fundamentalists are all about, but that means we don't have to do anything but sit here and bask in something that happened two thousand years ago."

The former priest felt strongly regarding church issues. He stated, "The Catholic Church is stuck in a lot of those kinds of ruts. The Church is now going back to earlier formal language in liturgy after having made a few small changes in the last ten or fifteen years. They claim to be going back to tradition." He regretted that "some ministers in established religions use tradition, ritual and dogma or the original scriptural language as a power base. They have enough followers who don't want to think for themselves that they get away with it. So it all becomes fixed instead of being open to change and to evolving."

Kelly believed the defining difference between traditional religion and progress in religion was that "traditional religious truth is fixed once and for all, but actually, religious progress should be a dynamic and evolving reality." He figured, "The God that I believe in put into this world the possibilities to continue to generate new and exciting things. Much organized religion has made a point of critiquing everything based on what Jesus said 2,000 years ago. But grains of truth from Jesus (and all the early prophets) need to be reinterpreted as history plays out."

For this author, Kelly listed progressive thoughts about Catholic Church sacraments and about the real purpose of ritual and liturgy:

The Eucharist (Communion): Kelly believed that when Jesus was coming to the end of his life, he knew:

> he was going to be destroyed and very aware it was about to happen. In Saint John's gospel, Jesus talks about all the things he stands for, all the things these apostles are supposed to do, their whole purpose and what's supposed to happen after he leaves. At the Last Supper, food is a binding force, a celebration, a family gathering, a symbol of togetherness. Jesus meant for us to regularly join together and share a meal. Share how you are doing and your spiritual progress. But suddenly we become literal 'This is my body' interpretation. Really Communion is a symbol of Jesus being present with the apostles. But having the bread transubstantiate, the Catholic

Church doctrine that the host actually physically changes into Jesus' body—who cares?

Continuing, Kelly said:

the Eucharist should be like a family meal. The Church language of Eucharist is so different from this. One line in there that I would never say is 'Lord I am not worthy.' Just before you are about to share the food you say, 'Lord I am not worthy?' What does that mean?

Relating to his actions at St. Mark's parish, Kelly added:

It actually was people coming together to reinforce themselves as people to live a decent life. On Holy Thursday, commemorating the supper the night before Jesus' crucifixion, the parish had their community space set up as a banquet hall, they'd go through the liturgy and then have a meal, which to Jesus, was the whole purpose. In treating Communion as a family meal, I was a renegade and I think I was a renegade in the right direction.

Regarding the rule that only Catholics at Mass can receive Communion, Kelly added, "If somebody is there who feels in the spirit, why would I say, 'I'm sorry, I can't give you this host?'"

Kelly, outspoken but devout in his beliefs, noted as the bread and wine were being prepared at Mass for Communion, the text of the prayer is "...the fruit of the vine and the work of human hands." John thought this symbolized our whole earthly role: "On one hand earth and vine, God will give us what we need. Our job is to work to make it productive and ongoing until the world ends. We need to take what God has given us, discover it, and use it for justice and good."

Baptism: Kelly said that he had been traditionally taught that the sacrament of Baptism was "about washing away original sin, our supposed moral congenital defect.... Catholic schools still teach that you are starting out defective based on the horrible things that went wrong with Adam and Eve, and only because of the grace of God [through Baptism] do you become healthy." Kelly instead thought God had made us correct from the start and gave us more opportunities to become healthy and whole. He did, however, favor the symbolism of life coming out of water. "Even Jesus talked about being reborn through water: he came out of the River Jordan water committed to the fullness of life. There are two different karma strains in the world: good and evil. You are born into a world with evil that you will be challenged by." Kelly believed that "through Baptism I come out of this living water to commit myself to living and resisting evil."

Confirmation: Kelly said it was important to notice how many cultures today have a ritual around reaching adolescence. "This is a reaffirming of the commitment to make spirituality part of your life now that you are old enough [about 14] to become aware of what life is all about and to gradually become independent." He thought the ritual "was beautiful if done right."

Matrimony: After leaving the priesthood, Kelly performed weddings as a Christian minister and as [an ordained online] Universal Life minister. He told couples, "You are marrying yourselves. I do not marry you—I only celebrate your commitment to one another. Your marriage is only valid if you have worked hard enough before you have come to the ceremony that you know who you are, what you want to do, and that you are really committed to sharing a life of love and growth." He asked four things of a couple: One, are you really communicating with each other? Two, how do you handle money? Three, how do you get along with your in-laws? And four, do you or don't you want to have kids? And is that a mutual decision? He brought that question up to a couple, and one said they didn't want kids and the other said they did. Kelly said, "Wait a minute, this conversation ceases right now. Go home, sit down, and figure out a mutual answer. If you get one, then come back; otherwise, forget it."

Kelly regretted that the Catholic Church decrees marriage as a sacrament for life, and if you divorce, you are forever evil "and thereafter you are condemned." Human nature being what it is, Kelly said, "I do everything I can when I marry a couple to be convinced that they have the basics of life ready to go, and they have indicated that they mean to stay together and be effective parents." Kelly allowed, however, that there was no guarantee that people were going to continue to grow together and share in this experience equally. Kelly believed one of the worst things that happens in the Catholic Church is that couples often stay together and live miserable lives because they fear the sin of divorce. Kelly didn't want a married couple staying together five or ten years after they realized they just didn't work as a couple. He told couples that "their relationship is more important than just having kids," and that having kids was not an excuse for staying together. Children cannot put it into words, but "kids know exactly what is going on when the marriage no longer works."

During the final few years that Kelly was a priest, when divorced people wanted to remarry, he would perform the wedding together with a Protestant minister so the couple would know that he was "still on their side" and did not support the prohibition of divorced Catholics remarrying.

Confession: "If a young person came in and didn't say he masturbated a few times and had dirty thoughts, I thought to myself, 'What's wrong with you, kid? Are you unhealthy?'" Kelly studied psychology so he could be more effective at understanding what people were telling him in confession and help them figure out some practical, real ways they could change if they wanted to. "I could tell them to say five Our Fathers and five Holy Marys and bless them, but they would be back in a week or two doing the same thing." Ideally, they would be able to sit down, "not necessarily in that cute little old confessional box, and actually have a conversation based on, '*Where are you coming from? What's going on? What do you see you need to change?*' And help put it into a life process for them." He continued, "Instead of just reacting to whatever is going on, whatever you are feeling, sit down and ask, what is the long-term effect if I keep doing this? And start changing the way you make decisions." Kelly said for penance to be effective within the church, it should be a way for people to "internalize what's going on and how they become better instead of just rattling off a bunch of prayers."

Sexuality: On other church issues, Kelly was not opposed to men choosing to be celibate as part of their priesthood if they understood what sexuality was and knew what they were doing. "But most of them don't understand enough to make an informed decision. A lot of the people my age who remain priests, those of us who were in the seminary in the forties and fifties, were not taught about sexuality. Most of the sexual crap (child abuse) that happened recently in the Catholic Church happened with priests who were around my age."

Kelly asked why the Church worries about homosexuality. "Give it up! Why fight it? If God is a God of love and he is responsible for this creation and he does everything for a purpose and for good, why does He make ten percent of humanity have an inclination to be homosexual instead of heterosexual? I defy anybody to tell me that a homosexual sets out to be homosexual. Who in the world would do that? My point is that God either made a mistake and therefore He is not this wonderful Being that we say He is, or there is a reason. I'm sorry; it makes no sense to me."

Kelly pointed to the Vatican under the leadership of Pope Benedict in 2012 trying to reign in the U.S. Catholic nuns for being too liberal, saying, "Well, the nuns are right on—their whole thing is about dealing with justice." He told this author of an article by his close friend from San Quentin Brian Cahill about Catholic bishops coming down on nuns for not following the rules. The Church is angry because "the nuns won't support the Church's ruling on abortion and sexuality and women being ministers." One line in the article is "exactly where I'm coming from—that is that the nuns are only interested in helping the poor and establishing justice."

Kelly thought nothing was worse than the power of "fuddy-duddy white priests" based on "pseudo spirituality." He was always uncomfortable when called "Father" by friends and former students. "That title is part of the power play and is brainwashing." Attaching and expressing that reverence to another ordinary human being "seems only a way to maintain religious status and authority. Does another human being other than one's blood father deserve that title? It seems to imply that the laity are in the child role in relation to a priest."

The former priest wasn't convinced the early Church thought that Jesus Christ was the *only* Son of God. That concept later became necessary for Christianity to tell the world that "we are 'Number One' and everybody else comes in second. If the Catholic Church doesn't change that attitude, it is not going to survive." Christianity's survival depends on "having people come together to talk about what Buddha, Mohammad, and other spiritual leaders of the world had to say. *'How do we connect?'* not *'How do we fight?'*" Kelly believed that interfaith communication was starting to happen and that Jesus and his message would comfortably fit into that scenario.

The Catholic Church has been, he said, "subject to Western and even Eastern influences and is now beginning to let women be real human beings when before they were servants or property." Kelly, as a priest, pointed to the passage from St. Paul's Epistle that wives must be submissive to their husbands: "Where did that come from? Jesus associated with women in opposition to his culture. He had women disciples."

⌇

Doctor Bill Schwartz of the Samaritan House free clinic told this author that he and Kelly discussed philosophy and religion at times. Kelly, of course, was Catholic, and Schwartz was Jewish. Schwartz said he never had experienced conversations with another person like those with Kelly. Schwartz said their views and perspectives were different, but they never resulted in anyone saying, "I'm right and you're wrong." Our discussion was mainly about how we can relate to others to make the world a better place; we decided we were doing it. He was doing it from his religious path, and I was doing it from my religious path, and both will lead to the same place. Both Catholicism and Judaism have service to humanity as a main tenet."

John Joseph Kelly 1928 - 2019: Monday, May 20, 2019, I stopped, ordered the usual medium chai latte and bear claw pastry to go, and walked the two blocks to our usual 8:30 a.m. John Kelly visit at San Mateo Leslie Towers. I arrived to see John's caregivers Tiki and Ruby, Pam Frisella, and nephew Patrick and got the sad news that John had died early that morning. They kindly allowed me a few minutes to pay my respects and feel his loss before the coroner came.

Celebration of life: A memorial service for John Kelly was held June 15, 2019 at 2 p.m. at Junipero Serra High School, 451 W. 20th Ave. in San Mateo. Pam Frisella and Patrick Kelly organized and acted as hosts for an auditorium filled with Kelly's friends and supporters. Congresswoman Jackie Speier, the keynote speaker, addressed an audience including local mayors, councilmembers, Kairos and Samaritan House volunteers, and a host of dignitaries. Kelly never sought acclaim or fame, but this huge gathering showed tremendous love and appreciation for this humble man. Many spoke of how John Kelly helped them succeed, sometimes against great odds. A few statements follow from before and after Kelly's life.

Comments about John Kelly

Pam Frisella (former mayor of Foster City): Of all the people this author interviewed, no one seemed closer to and more in touch with John Kelly than his longtime friend, Pam Frisella:

> John was unique and the most solely his own person of anybody I knew. He was the closest to being Jesus-like—and I told him this and he got all embarrassed—because he saw the need to feed the hungry and clothe the poor. John had few worldly goods, as we knew from cleaning out his apartment after his stroke. Material things meant absolutely nothing to this man. John had given the last five dollars out of his wallet but he didn't give the money so people would go away; he gave the money and then stayed until there was probably nothing more that he could do for that person.
>
> I mean he lived it; he walked the walk; he lived his beliefs. People thought he was not religious anymore because he was no longer a Catholic priest but that was far from the truth because Jesus was still his leader. He had done everything the way that he thought Jesus wanted him to do it. And he stayed with it. People might help others once in a while, and then they'll go to the spa instead of giving a hundred dollars to the poor.

Kelly took Frisella to San Quentin, and she worked a couple of Kairos teams with him. He opened up another part of Frisella's life. She said, "I would have never seen this except by talking to lifers who can be delightful human beings, who just because they made that one mistake in their life now have to pay for it."

For six earlier years, Frisella had thrown birthday parties for Kelly:

> The events became reunions for the parolees he had helped. As Mayor of Foster City at the time, I told the police 'not to run any plates' (check license plates against criminal data bases) on the Saturday night of the party because the parolee guests were not here illegally. This last November before he died, we had about forty people; they brought their spouses and a couple brought their kids. They worship Kelly because he had been their advocate. He never ever gave up on them.

Years ago, Red Moroney Sr., Red Moroney, Janet Jones, Dolores Kelly-Hons, and Frisella had had a little bit of a social group going with Kelly as an active member. They would go dancing someplace in Foster City, California. Frisella said these group meetings helped her see a different side of John:

> I wished that he could have known a romantic love. When Kelly was in assisted living in Burlingame recovering from his stroke, he made a comment to me one day that made me really,

really sad. They had a little music group playing love songs on Kelly's TV. The onlookers included obvious widows who were looking kind
of melancholy. You could tell they were reliving
memories, and Kelly said that then he realized
that he had never had a relationship. I thought
it must have had to do with twenty-five years
in the priesthood and after that maybe he had
a fear of getting into a relationship. I remember
that there were a few women who were after him
when he headed Samaritan House. But he did
not want to become involved with anybody in
a romantic way.

Frisella believed Kelly gradually became more aware of how
he missed the personal connections from when he was a priest:

When he had Church services everyone came
forward. The attention and help he got after
his stroke in December 2011 reminded him
that attention felt pretty good. During his initial stroke recovery, he'd say that there were
just so many visitors that he didn't even answer
the phone. But he counted how many people
stopped in that day. Even though he sounded
like he was annoyed he really wasn't. Then all
of a sudden, the attention fell off again, because
people thought he was OK. People emailed me
and asked how Kelly was doing and I gave them
his home number and said, 'Why don't you call

him?' That was the message we had to communicate to people.

Patrick Kelly (John Kelly's nephew and maybe his closest relative):

It had always been fun Uncle John—not Father John the Priest. He was always around and he played with us and had wonderful patience. John seemed to relish being the cool uncle. Each year he gave me and my sisters an *experience* gift: whatever we wanted to do in the Bay area with Kelly. He would take us to Great America; Marine World; a ferry ride to Angel Island. It was always fun. John relished the fact that he was letting us kids be kids.

John for the forty plus years I've known him has been nothing but selfless; I think of all the things he did for us growing up; and for the community—the kids at PAL and those folks at San Quentin. His whole life had been about giving.

Although selfless, John fought with himself over his machismo and his ego; he beat himself down if he felt like he was getting a little too big for his britches. John was not perfect but instead tried hard to do the right thing every day. He was not a Mother Theresa but someone who was really trying to figure things out. The Bible provides wonderful examples of how to live like Christ but in my case, I got more from watching John than from any written word.

Patrick and Pam organized John's post-stroke apartment clean-out and discovered a snapshot of what matters to John and what doesn't:

> He had a probably thirty-year-old mattress on the floor, hand-me-down couches, and end tables that were probably ten, fifteen, twenty years old *before* he received them from his parents. They had some utility and that's all he needed; it was good enough for him. As a humble person, worldly trappings were not important. But what did matter was every single letter he received from someone, especially those from San Quentin and materials from Kairos, which were all stacked up on the kitchen table.

Patrick brought Kelly back to San Quentin eight weeks after his stroke, and "he received a massive standing ovation in the prison church when the priest welcomed him back. It was very touching for him." An African-American inmate later said to Patrick, "One thing I absolutely loved about John Kelly is that, from the first time that I met him, the color of my skin never mattered. From the first time I met him he was my brother."

Elaine Leeder (Dean Emerita of the School of Social Sciences and Professor Emerita of Sociology at Sonoma State University and author *of My Life with Lifers***; co-led with John Kelly a San Quentin program, "New Leaf on Life"):**

I was blown away by how the men in prison responded to him. He looked like a rock star around the San Quentin campus, a university except that everyone is locked up. Everybody knew him—across the yard, 'John, John, John'—they all wanted to talk to him. He couldn't move more than a few feet and somebody else approached him to tell him about this and about that. I thought this is a remarkable man because he is so well liked. I started to work with him and began to see John's humanity, as a decent and generous soul. He embraced people as they are, not for what they did. And he saw the good in every human being. And the guys responded to that; they really saw that he respected and loved them in the full sense of his Christian background. I am Jewish, but saw Catholic John and totally understood what it was like for somebody to truly live a spiritual Christian life.

Leeder told this author she was:

thrilled that John was being honored by his story being told because he was a remarkable man. A biography is a way of cloning him; some way of noting what he has done. And some, hopefully, will pick up his example. There is good and evil in this world and John is good. He found the spark of humanity in each person and the rest of us should model that.

Sue Lempert (former San Mateo, CA Mayor):

John typically didn't talk much at Rotary Club but one day he talked about why he left the priesthood. He wasn't kicked out. Just moral reasons are why he did it. So, if there was any real follower of Jesus, it was John. He really cared about the disadvantaged; he really did. Not for political reasons or anything else. He was a wonderful human being.

Brian Cahill (worked with John for years at San Quentin):

Yes, John could be crusty and cantankerous but most of us knew it was really an act. While he would have been the last person in the world to have seen himself as a saint, I believe he was, perhaps not in the tradition of canonized saints (he would have turned it down if it had come from the official church), but more along the lines of Dorothy Day. Like her, John lived his life with a passion for charity, justice, and a full-bore commitment to the poor, marginalized, and vulnerable among us.

Walter Heyman (active Samaritan House Board member):

I once asked John why he left the priesthood and was told he left the Church—but not Christianity, 'because the Church of that day was trying to solve present-day problems with medieval methods.'

Susan Manheimer (former San Mateo and Oakland, CA Chief of Police):

John touched so many young people, but he was a personification of all the Ten Commandments and of all our great social values. Kelly would tell you, 'I'm no saint,' and, 'I'm not involved in this as a mission. I'm just merely doing what I was put here to do.' He had this innate sense of helping those most in need.

Tom Brady, Sr.:

I've been blessed to know John Kelly for 45 years.... He has been one of the most influential treasures in my life and...in the lives of... people from all the different backgrounds where he traveled.

John Kelly was a collector and influencer of people because...he talked, supported and loved them. (He had) limited means except for his overflowing heart of love that he extended to all who he encouraged. John changed the lives of so many people that he (was)...the "Godfather of the Peninsula."

...as a priest at Serra, a private counselor...a driving force of Samaritan House and in the last chapter of his life...counselor at San Quentin

Prison, John profoundly impacted the very existence of those he encountered.

Speaking for myself and my family, we are extremely thankful that we were honored to be his friend.

Warren Blank, PhD, (President and CEO of LeadershipGroup.com)

John Kelly was a true leader, with courage and commitment to help others help themselves.

As John Calvin Maxwell succinctly stated: "To add value to others, one must first value others." John Kelly's legacy will be his compassion; his devotion to the physical, emotional and psychological healing of the socially and racially disadvantaged is a beautiful model to guide us all through these uncertain and troubled times.

Jerry Forbes (Samaritan House supporter and fellow Kairos team member):

John was very focused. He got things done that you never thought would happen. But all of a sudden, he'd have people on his side and to this day you didn't know how it happened. Samaritan House was an example. There were not many people particularly interested. It was a struggle to get people together to start doing the

Samaritan House work. He knew how to attract the right people.

Kelly was a sometimes-cranky old man who had a heart of gold. He didn't show it but did it in his actions. Kelly said, 'Don't praise me.' But he was doing things he needed to be praised for. What little money he had he often used to help someone else. The man was a giver.

Jerry Hill (California State Senator):

John Kelly committed his life to helping those less fortunate. He was a role model for the community, an exemplary citizen, and he sensitized so many of us to the plight of our fellows. Our community was better because of John Kelly.

Dr. Bill Schwartz (Samaritan House Board member and free clinic advocate):

John was a natural leader. I would follow him anywhere he told me to go and not that many people had that effect on me. He was very persuasive. He was fully involved himself. And that was why he was so successful building the Samaritan House organization over the years. He worked well with people and in particular he had motivational skills. He was the head dog, the alpha male. We followed him and it was always a pleasure.

Jeanne Elliott (former Bayside Academy Middle School principal):

> Forgiveness and humanity were the themes of John's work and these had been emblematic in all efforts of John Kelly. He accepted us for who we were and helped us do good deeds without giving us a hard time about our failings.

Red Moroney (former student of Kelly and Kairos team member):

> John and Kairos were very successful at San Quentin in particular. In fact, recidivism rates of people who have been through the Kairos program are like thirty-six or thirty-seven percent as opposed to the general population which is about seventy-seven percent. The Kairos program was starting to attract the attention of the administration and people in the corrections field.

Hope Whipple Williams (original Samaritan House agency director):

> John knew how important it was for teens to be successful adults and mentored many children, youth, and teens over his years. He was compassionate, caring, and like the Energizer Bunny, he kept going and going in spite of his health issues. John is a legend in the greater San Mateo

Community and we could never repay him for his services over the years.

Don Kelly (John's brother):

John took great pride in his dedicated work and accomplishments for the underprivileged. He had a sincere heart and concern for the down-trodden, and he applied this concern in loving commitment every single day of his life.

JOHN KELLY ON JOHN KELLY AND THIS BOOK

During one of the conversations with this author, John said he was nervous about this biography being published because he was trying "to keep my ego under control." He struggled with little self-confidence as a youth and low self-esteem, even depression, after leaving his church. He said the lifestyle of being a priest left out a lot of humanity, and "when you try to put life back together after priesthood, it is really a challenge." And he worried that he was getting old and couldn't remember all that was necessary for a biography. But he did remember many "great adventures."

He said, "If we are getting anything out of this biography process, it should be to develop a sense of the need to really move beyond a lot of the aspects of our culture like greed and selfishness and competition to the point where we realize our basic purpose is to help one another. The most important thing you can do is help another human being." Kelly saw so many people who had ability, and he wanted to see those abilities blossom. That's what drove him.

Kelly believed that in the current age of mass media and enhanced connection with each other, our main responsibility was to "compare notes and to come to the common understanding of who we are. We should avoid saying to other cultures, 'I got it right, you got it wrong; either believe it my way or you are never going to make it to heaven.'"

And for our local community responsibility, he said, "You help the kids before they get in trouble. You help them think about who they are and what they want to become. The guys in San Quentin screwed up in their youth, but some are at the point where they think about who they are and who they want to be. In many ways, inmates are delayed adolescents. Practically speaking, the earlier you can have people rethinking the better."

John Kelly claimed that he had the same feeling when he walked into San Quentin prison as when he taught at Serra High School. Many inmates stopped and said hello and gave John a slap on the back. He felt that he experienced a lot of unconditional love in that building. He said if they tried to thank him, he'd say, "Forget it. I'm getting a payoff here, buddy. I don't need your thanks."

Former Serra High School Principal Mike
Peterson, John Kelly, and author—2013.

Kelly's 88th birthday with Congresswoman Jackie Speier.

John Kelly Memorial.

AUTHOR'S NOTE

Some may ask why I chose to write a biography of John Joseph Kelly. Here is part of my reasoning for doing so and what made me believe that people around the world should know about this remarkable man.

John began teaching at Serra High School in San Mateo, California in 1956, my sophomore year at Notre Dame High School in Niles, Illinois. As a poor student and troublemaker, I would have been a regular attendee at Father Kelly's "jug" (after-school detention). Like John, I was raised Catholic and held firm the religious cards dealt to me by my family and church.

In 1968, John, back from Notre Dame University enlightenment, had his defining moment and left Serra High School. I had my parallel defining moment in Vietnam that year as I questioned my military career and even my government as I became acutely aware of political jingoism and lies about our foreign wars. I fulfilled my five year naval aviator contract and exited the military in January 1970. Shortly thereafter, I left my religion. John and I both left the Catholic Church in the 1970s, opting for alternate spiritual choices.

John as a priest had much more at stake than I did, but I did relate to his separation anxiety. At a single Sunday Mass I decided to reject rigid church dogma; I could no longer be a Catholic. I stepped anxiously into a religious vacuum of thirty years until revisiting my own spirituality in the form of my book, *Spiritual Choices: Putting the HERE in Hereafter*. John and I had each decided that how we act toward others was far more important than what we were told to believe in church and that we didn't need formal religion to be spiritual.

Never having had the same capacity to work with society's disadvantaged as John, I hoped instead to support his life works by spreading word of his advocacy and helping to advance his passion for compassion and for restorative justice. My goal is to leverage his voice and expand the discussion about religious and especially criminal justice reform. John worked on an organizational level, but he was no policy wonk. He was mostly a one-on-one, hands-on person. His individual approach, though, led to broader consideration of prison and parole reform.

A guiding principle for enlightened social and government leaders is that preventing social ills is more effective than trying to cure them later. Yet the bulk of public budget money goes to after-the-fact cure—cure in the hospital, cure in the jail. Shouldn't we instead as a society allocate much of that same money to prevention of the causes of poverty and crime?

This is what John had in mind working with troubled youth and creating better conditions for all people in our communities. People generally do not dispute that prevention of poverty and crime would be effective and, if that were our emphasis, our society would be better off long-term. However, there are important special interests: law enforcement, prison guards, judges, welfare workers, homeless advocates—people whose jobs depend primarily on the curative approach as opposed to prevention. While it would undoubtedly be a challenge to make that quantum shift of funds, where our tax money goes is really where our community goals are.

I had been involved in local government at a policy level for many years and believed the public sector's first job is maintaining and enhancing public safety. Stated simply, I believe dangerous criminals should be locked up to keep them from harming others. However, many politicians have played to the public's fears, sometimes obscuring the simple truth that the great majority of prison and jail inmates will eventually rejoin their communities. If those inmates have been merely warehoused, will we as a community be safer when they are released? Not likely!

There is a great deal we don't know about criminal acts and the criminal mind. We know little about brain chemistry and the nature of evil. We do know good people sometimes come from horrible circumstances but that more often, poor social conditions produce poor social results. Inner city slums produce more crime than affluent suburbs. Is science now capable of predicting who will commit serious crime? Will it ever be?

A prime question for Americans and especially for Californians is why we still have so many people in jail and prison. Can we bear that cost when the alternative might be funding education or improving the broad general health of our neighborhoods? Are we safer having so many nonviolent people locked up in prison?

These are not just questions for criminal justice experts and politicos. We as ordinary citizens with good information and relevant choices can also come to reasonable and workable conclusions. Kelly's case is not going to provide statistical analysis or proof, but he did show us what success looks like, at least in some important individual cases.

I'm no criminal justice expert, but as a parent and grandparent, I feel responsible for helping to make our social environment safer, even if just by a little bit. Beyond telling John's story, I advocate taking a closer look at victimless crime and drug, alcohol, and mental health policies and their measured effects. We need to review the California and national parole policy and analyze the unintended social and economic ill effects of technical violations not associated with a new crime. Those violations sometimes put people back in jail, often disrupting their families and jobs. Unneeded and unaffordable pre-trial bail causes the same disruption. Excessive incarceration is expensive and crowds out funding for other public safety.

John Kelly was not about cost/benefit ratios and analytic studies. What he was about was demonstrating the good that comes from showing responsible adult attention to young potential teen gang members. He knew that even among people who have done wrong, at least some are willing to change and become assets to society. John worked on helping inmates find their own cure, and he helped them and us prevent future criminal activity. He was mostly about helping one more person find the good in himself. Compassion and forgiveness were his watchwords.

I once compared John to Jesus, but that seemed not exactly right. But if you think of the good works and social change Jesus brought to his world as a holy man rather than as God, the comparison feels better. I believe John accepted his responsibility to make the best use of the gifts given to us generally and especially to him personally to do unto others as he would have them do unto him. Jesus seemed not so much about the outward prayer and devotion of his Jewish heritage as he was about physically helping the poor and disadvantaged in his world. Kelly did that in our world. His joy came from doing the meaningful work of helping others.

I have shared John's life lessons and have learned in the process. Following the action-oriented life examples of Jesus and many of the world's great spiritual leaders has served Kelly and his community well. Kelly's life is a testament to not only racial and economic equality, but also to the acceptance, love, and compassion that will help us reach our full human potential.

While others prayed, he provided.

Your comments are welcome at: www.spiritualchoices.com

ACKNOWLEDGMENTS

To: John Kelly for reluctantly agreeing to his biography so his story could be told and for his myriad of friends interviewed for this book.